MUSIC THEORY WORKBOOK

FOR ALL MUSICIANS

A self-study course with illustrations & examples
for you to write & check your answers

BY CHRIS BOWMAN

ISBN 978-1-4768-0852-9

HAL•LEONARD®

7777 W. BLUEMOUND RD. P.O. BOX 13819 MILWAUKEE, WI 53213

In Australia Contact:
Hal Leonard Australia Pty. Ltd.
4 Lentara Court
Cheltenham, Victoria, 3192 Australia
Email: ausadmin@halleonard.com.au

Visit Hal Leonard Online at
www.halleonard.com

CONTENTS

PART TWO: HARMONY, INTERVALS & CHORD STRUCTURE

PREFACE

Music theory, in all its complexities, is a wonderful and exciting area of essential study for all musicians who participate – or wish to participate – in mastering soloing, arranging, orchestrating, writing or composing, copying, ear training, communicating with other musicians, or any other fun, creative, or imaginative undertaking in the world of music.

This book is targeted for the intermediate player for any instrument. You should have a knowledge of the treble clef, chromatics, how to identify all notes on your instrument (For guitar, this means identifying all notes on all strings, all frets.) if you are to gain maximum benefit from your efforts. It would also be helpful to know a few scale forms or positions and some basic major, minor, seventh, ninth chords, etc. Get a chord book and scale book if necessary, and use this to enhance what you are gaining from your studies here. If you are not yet at this level, I suggest that you locate an instructor in your area to help with the essential rudiments.

The essence of this book is the study of major and minor scales, key signatures, chords, progressions, chord substitutions, and ear training. I briefly mention some altered scales and modes, but there is very little material about them in this book. For rhythm studies, many study books are available from your local music store or online.

This book is a workbook. Contained herein are the essential basic **backbone** concepts for the working musician. These are the things you **must** know. It may take a year to work through and thoroughly understand and memorize all that is in this book – and a lifetime to perfect it. That's okay. You will own it and never forget it.

HOW TO USE THIS BOOK

For all useful purposes and for thorough understanding, music theory must be written down by hand, usually several times. Space is provided in this book for you to write the assignments, but you may wish to obtain an extra manuscript book to perfect your craft if the space here is not sufficient for your writing practice. **Always write in pencil**, so you can correct your mistakes. Answers are in the back of the book.

Always follow this sequence for complete understanding. Repeat each step as often as needed. It is suggested that you have a complete understanding of each key before you proceed to the next.

10 STEPS TO LEARNING THEORY

1. Know the formula.
2. Write it.
3. Apply the key signature.
4. Play it.
5. Listen to it (repeatedly).
6. Analyze it.
7. Verbalize it.
8. Memorize it.
9. Quiz it.
10. Review it.

In music theory, **everything is important**. Memorize all of it! As long as you have to review notes or books to answer questions you may encounter, you have not absorbed the material. Not until all is memorized will you have command of the wonderful tools that music theory will provide you.

- It is the intensive study over periods of time that gets results. Each lesson or new item should be repeated until the light comes on.
- Work one key at a time, one chord at a time. Be patient. When your brain is full, take a break.
- Promise yourself that you will complete this book. Rest assured that all aspects of your playing, understanding, and communicating will improve by 100 percent or more. Isn't that exciting? I remember when the light came on for me. I was so excited! Up until that point, I had a lot of info, but it wasn't connected. Wait until it connects for you. You won't be sorry.

PART ONE
SCALES

MAJOR SCALES
THE SHARP KEYS

This section will teach you how to build major scales. Each major scale consists of eight notes (or degrees) in each octave, beginning at the first scale degree (also called the **tonic** or the **tonal center**). We will use the treble clef exclusively. You can transpose the bass clef if needed.

We'll begin with the simplest of the major scales, C major.

LESSON 1 — C MAJOR SCALE

Step 1: Formula

All intervals, or distances between notes will be a full step, except for the third and fourth degrees, and the seventh and eighth degrees, which will be a half step. (On the guitar, a half step is one fret and a whole step is two frets. On the piano, a half step is from a white note to the adjacent black note, except for E-F and B-C, which are from white note to white note.)

Note: The natural half steps of E-F and B-C happen to occur in just the right places for the C major scale below, as well as do all of the other natural notes.

As we verbalize the process:

C to D is a whole step; 1-2 should be a whole step, no change to make.

D to E is a whole step; 2-3 should be a whole step, no change to make.

E to F is a half step; 3-4 should be a half step, no change to make.

F to G is a whole step; 4-5 should be a whole step, no change to make.

G to A is a whole step; 5-6 should be a whole step, no change to make.

A to B is a whole step; 6-7 should be a whole step, no change to make.

B to C is a half step; 7-8 should be a half step, no change to make.

All the natural notes occur in such a way that there are no changes or alterations, called accidentals, to make. We say that **the key signature for C major is no sharps, no flats**, all natural notes. What happens in this octave happens in all octaves, either up or down.

Now write below the C major scale in one octave. Be sure to number the degrees and place parentheses around the (3-4) and the (7-8) to remind you where the half steps occur. The first and the eighth are octaves, both Cs. So, in terms of repeating notes in the second octave:

- 8 = 1 8va (up one octave)
- 9 = 2 8va
- 10 = 3 8va
- 11 = 4 8va
- 12 = 5 8va
- 13 = 6 8va
- 14 = 7 8va
- 15 = 1 15ma (up two octaves)

These comparisons will become evident as we explore the other scales, keys, and chords.

Step 2: Write it.

C major scale

Step 3: Key signature for C major is no sharps, no flats.

In keeping with our plan:

Step 4: Play it.

Step 5: Listen to it.

Step 6: Analyze it.

Step 7: Verbalize it.

Step 8: Memorize it.

Stop here until you have done all of the above. Play it in as many octaves as you can. TIP: After you play it thinking notes, play it thinking intervals. In other words place all notes a whole step apart except the third and fourth and the seventh and eighth. Work it now.

Remember: Once you become skilled with this, you can start on any note in the scale, not always on the tonic note. The trick is to remember exactly what degree you are on at the time – and where the half steps occur.

Step 9:

QUIZ 1

1. What is the first degree of C major?_____
   Find as many as you can on your instrument, in all octaves.

2. What is the third degree?_____ *Find as many as you can.*

3. What is the fifth degree?_____ *Find as many as you can.*

4. What is the seventh degree?_____ *Find as many as you can.*

5. What is the fourth degree?_____ *Find as many as you can.*

6. What is the second degree?_____ *Find as many as you can.*

7. What is the sixth degree?_____ *Find as many as you can.*

8. What is the key signature for C major? _____ *Find as many as you can.*

Now play in this order: 1-3-5-7 in one octave, then in two octaves.

Memorize this. We will see this formula over and over again.

This lesson will take one or two days of work, or perhaps a week if you have only a few minutes a day to work on it. Make sure that you thoroughly understand it before you proceed to the next lesson.

Step 10: Review all you have done so far.

LESSON 2 — G MAJOR SCALE

Step 1: Apply the formula (3-4 and 7-8 half steps, all others whole steps).

Step 2: Write the G major scale below.

Be sure to number all degrees, with (3-4) and (7-8) in parentheses. Verbalize the process as we did in C major on page 3. You should end up with all natural notes, except for the seventh degree, which is F♯.

Step 3: Key signature for G major is F♯.

In keeping with our plan:

Step 4: Play it.

Step 5: Listen to it.

Step 6: Analyze it.

Step 7: Verbalize it.

Step 8: Memorize it.

Step 9:

QUIZ 2

1. What is the first degree of G major?_____ *Find as many as you can.*

2. What is the third degree?_____ *Find as many as you can.*

3. What is the fifth degree?_____ *Find as many as you can.*

4. What is the seventh degree?_____ *Find as many as you can.*

5. What is the fourth degree?_____ *Find as many as you can.*

6. What is the second degree?_____ *Find as many as you can.*

7. What is the sixth degree?_____ *Find as many as you can.*

8. What is the key signature for G major? _____

Now play in this order: 1-3-5-7 in one octave, then in two octaves.

Memorize this lesson in its entirety before proceeding to the next lesson.

Step 10: Review G major.

LESSON 3 — D MAJOR SCALE

Step 1: Formula

Step 2: Write the D major scale below.

Bracket (3-4) and (7-8). Verbalize the process as we did in the last two lessons.

Step 3: What is the key signature for D major?_____

In keeping with our plan:

Step 4: Play it.

Step 5: Listen to it.

Step 6: Analyze it.

Step 7: Verbalize it.

Step 8: Memorize it.

Step 9:

QUIZ 3

1. What is the first degree of D major?_____ *Find as many as you can.*

2. What is the third degree?_____ *Find as many as you can.*

3. What is the fifth degree?_____ *Find as many as you can.*

4. What is the seventh degree?_____ *Find as many as you can.*

5. What is the fourth degree?_____ *Find as many as you can.*

6. What is the second degree?_____ *Find as many as you can.*

7. What is the sixth degree?_____ *Find as many as you can.*

8. What is the key signature for D major? _____

Now play in order 1-3-5-7 in one octave, then in two octaves.

Memorize this lesson before proceeding to the next lesson.

Step 10: Review D major.

LESSON 4 — A MAJOR SCALE

Step 1: Formula

Step 2: Write the A major scale below.

Bracket (3-4) and (7-8). Verbalize the process as we did in the previous lessons.

Step 3: What is the key signature for A major? _____

Do you notice a predictable process evolving?

In keeping with our plan:

Step 4: Play it.

Step 5: Listen to it.

Step 6: Analyze it.

Step 7: Verbalize it.

Step 8: Memorize it.

Step 9:

QUIZ 4

1. What is the first degree of A major?_____ *Find them all.*

2. What is the third degree?_____ *Find them all.*

3. What is the fifth degree?_____ *Find them all.*

4. What is the seventh degree?_____ *Find them all.*

5. What is the fourth degree?_____ *Find them all.*

6. What is the second degree?_____ *Find them all.*

7. What is the sixth degree?_____ *Find them all.*

8. What is the key signature for A major?_____

Now play in order 1-3-5-7 in one octave, then in two octaves.

Step 10: Review A major.

LESSON 5 — E MAJOR SCALE

Step 1: Formula

Step 2: Write the E major scale below.

Bracket (3-4) and (7-8). Verbalize the process as we did in the previous lessons.

Step 3: What is the key signature for E major?_____

Step 4: Play it.

Step 5: Listen to it.

Step 6: Analyze it.

Step 7: Verbalize it.

Step 8: Memorize it.

Step 9:

QUIZ 5

1. What is the first degree of E major?_____ *Find them all.*

2. What is the third degree?_____ *Find them all.*

3. What is the fifth degree?_____ *Find them all.*

4. What is the seventh degree?_____ *Find them all.*

5. What is the fourth degree?_____ *Find them all.*

6. What is the second degree?_____ *Find them all.*

7. What is the sixth degree?_____ *Find them all.*

8. What is the key signature for E major? _____

9. What is the key signature for A major? _____

10. What is the key signature for D major? _____

11. What is the key signature for G major? _____

12. What is the key signature for C major? _____

Now play in E the 1-3-5-7, first in one octave, then in two.

Step 10: Review E major.

LESSON 6 — B MAJOR SCALE

Step 1: Formula

Step 2: Write the B major scale below.

Bracket (3-4) and (7-8). Verbalize the process.

Step 3: What is the key signature for B major?_____

You should have five sharps.

Step 4: Play it.

Step 5: Listen to it.

Step 6: Analyze it.

Step 7: Verbalize it.

Step 8: Memorize it.

Step 9:

QUIZ 6

1. What is the first degree of B major?_____ *Find them all.*

2. What is the third degree?_____ *Find them all.*

3. What is the fifth degree?_____ *Find them all.*

4. What is the seventh degree?_____ *Find them all.*

5. What is the fourth degree?_____ *Find them all.*

6. What is the second degree?_____ *Find them all.*

7. What is the sixth degree?_____ *Find them all.*

8. What is the key signature for B major? _____

Now play in E the 1-3-5-7, first in one octave, then in two.

Step 10: Review B major.

Take heart! There are only two more sharp keys.

LESSON 7 — F♯ MAJOR SCALE

Step 1: Formula

Step 2: Write the F♯ major scale below.

Bracket (3-4) and (7-8). Verbalize the process.

Step 3: What is the key signature for F♯ major? _____

Step 4: Play it.

Step 5: Listen to it.

Step 6: Analyze it.

Step 7: Verbalize it.

Step 8: Memorize it.

Step 9:

QUIZ 7

1. What is the first degree of F♯ major?_____ *Find them all.*

2. What is the third degree?_____ *Find them all.*

3. What is the fifth degree?_____ *Find them all.*

4. What is the seventh degree?_____ *Find them all.*

5. What is the fourth degree?_____ *Find them all.*

6. What is the second degree?_____ *Find them all.*

7. What is the sixth degree?_____ *Find them all.*

8. What is the key signature for F♯ major? _____

Now play the 1-3-5-7, first in one octave, then in two.

Step 10: Review F♯ major.

LESSON 8 — C♯ MAJOR SCALE

Step 1: Formula

Step 2: Write the C♯ major scale below.

Bracket (3-4) and (7-8). Verbalize the process.

Step 3: What is the key signature for C♯ major? _____

Step 4: Play it.

Step 5: Listen to it.

Step 6: Analyze it.

Step 7: Verbalize it.

Step 8: Memorize it.

Step 9:

QUIZ 8

1. What is the first degree of C♯ major?_____ *Find them all.*

2. What is the third degree?_____ *Find them all.*

3. What is the fifth degree?_____ *Find them all.*

4. What is the seventh degree?_____ *Find them all.*

5. What is the fourth degree?_____ *Find them all.*

6. What is the second degree?_____ *Find them all.*

7. What is the sixth degree?_____ *Find them all.*

8. What is the key signature for C♯ major? _____

9. What is the key signature for F♯ major? _____

10. What is the key signature for B major? _____

11. What is the key signature for E major? _____

12. What is the key signature for A major? _____

13. What is the key signature for D major? _____

14. What is the key signature for G major? _____

15. What is the key signature for C major? _____

Now in C♯ major, play the 1-3-5-7 in one octave, then in two.

Step 10: Review C♯ major.

If you could answer all of the above questions correctly without having to review any material, you have done well. If you had to review, that's okay, but it should let you know that you still have some work to do here.

THE CIRCLE OF FIFTHS

A pattern developed as you constructed the sharp keys, didn't it? Sharp keys move in what is called the **Circle of Fifths**. From the key of C major (no sharps, no flats), go to the fifth. It is G, right? That happens to be the next key to build. When you constructed it, you picked up one sharp: the seventh note, an F♯. Now go to the fifth of G, it is a D. That is your new key. Notice that you sharped the seventh note (C♯), and kept the F♯ you picked up in G major. As you proceed through the circle, you keep all previous sharped notes, and the new sharp is **always** the seventh. You will also observe that the order in which the sharps appear on the staff follows the Circle of Fifths.

The sequence goes like this:

C major (no sharps, no flats)
G major (F♯)
D major (F♯, C♯)
A major (F♯, C♯, G♯)
E major (F♯, C♯, G♯, D♯)
B major (F♯, C♯, G♯, D♯, A♯)
F♯ major (F♯, C♯, G♯, D♯, A♯, E♯)
C♯ major (F♯, C♯, G♯, D♯, A♯, E♯, B♯)

Note: In the keys of F♯ major and C♯ major, E♯ sounds and looks like F, and B♯ sounds and looks like C. We call these **enharmonic** spellings.

Look in the Answer Section of this book for an example of each major scale (page 96).

At this juncture, you may have had your fill of major scales and wish to use some of your knowledge to create harmony. If so, proceed to Part Two: Harmony, Intervals & Chord Structure (page 49).

Section B continues with the **major scale flat keys** in the same context and format as Section A, which we just finished. If you wish to proceed to Part Two, don't forget that all of Section B must be finished also.

MAJOR SCALES
THE FLAT KEYS

Flat keys move in a **Circle of Fourths**. As you proceed, notice that after F major (with one flat, B♭), we go to the next scale (B♭), and each successive key adds the new fourth degree as flat, and so on. The order in which the flats appear also follows the Circle of Fourths.

LESSON 9 — F MAJOR SCALE

Step 1: Formula (same as in the previous section on major scales).

Step 2: Write the F major scale below.

Step 3: What is the key signature? The fourth degree is a B♭.
All others are natural.

Step 4: Play it.

Step 5: Listen to it.

Step 6: Analyze it.

Step 7: Verbalize it.

Step 8: Memorize it.

Step 9:

QUIZ 9

1. What is the first degree of F major? _____

2. What is the third? _____

3. What is the fifth? _____

4. What is the seventh? _____

5. What is the fourth? _____

6. What is the second? _____

7. What is the sixth? _____

8. What is the key signature for F major? _____

Remember to find all reiterations of each scale degree up and down the positions of your instrument.

Now play the 1-3-5-7 in every octave.

Step 10: Review F major.

LESSON 10 — B♭ MAJOR SCALE

Step 1: Formula

Step 2: Write the B♭ major scale below. (Hint: Flat the first and last notes before you start. Both are B♭.)

Step 3: What is the key signature? _____

Step 4: Play it.

Step 5: Listen to it.

Step 6: Analyze it.

Step 7: Verbalize it.

Step 8: Memorize it.

Step 9:

QUIZ 10

1. What is the first degree of B♭ major? _____ *Find them all.*

2. What is the third?_____

3. What is the fifth? _____

4. What is the seventh? _____

5. What is the fourth? _____

6. What is the second? _____

7. What is the sixth? _____

8. What is the key signature for B♭ major? _____

Play the 1-3-5-7 in every octave on your instrument.

Step 10: Review B♭ major.

LESSON 11 — E♭ MAJOR SCALE

Step 1: Formula

Step 2: Write the E♭ major scale below.

Step 3: What is the key signature? _____

Step 4: Play it.

Step 5: Listen to it.

Step 6: Analyze it.

Step 7: Verbalize it.

Step 8: Memorize it.

Step 9:

QUIZ 11

1. What is the first degree of E♭ major? _____ *Find them all.*

2. What is the third?_____

3. What is the fifth?_____

4. What is the seventh?_____

5. What is the fourth?_____

6. What is the second?_____

7. What is the sixth?_____

8. What is the key signature for E♭ major?_____

Play the 1-3-5-7 in every octave on your instrument.

Step 10: Review E♭ major.

LESSON 12 – A♭ MAJOR SCALE

Step 1: Formula

Step 2: Write the A♭ major scale below.

Step 3: What is the key signature? _____

Step 4: Play it.

Step 5: Listen to it.

Step 6: Analyze it.

Step 7: Verbalize it.

Step 8: Memorize it.

Step 9:

QUIZ 12

1. What is the first degree of A♭ major? _____ *Find them all.*

2. What is the third?_____

3. What is the fifth?_____

4. What is the seventh?_____

5. What is the fourth?_____

6. What is the second?_____

7. What is the sixth?_____

8. What is the key signature for A♭ major?_____

Play the 1-3-5-7 in every octave on your instrument.

Step 10: Review A♭ major.

LESSON 13 – D♭ MAJOR SCALE

Step 1: Formula

Step 2: Write the D♭ major scale below.

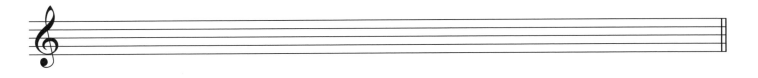

Step 3: What is the key signature? _____

Step 4: Play it.

Step 5: Listen to it.

Step 6: Analyze it.

Step 7: Verbalize it.

Step 8: Memorize it.

Step 9:

QUIZ 13

1. What is the first degree of D♭ major? _____ *Find them all.*

2. What is the third?_____

3. What is the fifth?_____

4. What is the seventh?_____

5. What is the fourth?_____

6. What is the second?_____

7. What is the sixth?_____

8. What is the key signature for D♭ major?_____

Play the 1-3-5-7 in every octave on your instrument.

Step 10: Review D♭ major.

LESSON 14 – G♭ MAJOR SCALE

Step 1: Formula

Step 2: Write the G♭ major scale below.

Step 3: What is the key signature? _____

Step 4: Play it.

Step 5: Listen to it.

Step 6: Analyze it.

Step 7: Verbalize it.

Step 8: Memorize it.

Step 9:

QUIZ 14

1. What is the first degree of G♭ major? _____ *Find them all.*

2. What is the third?_____

3. What is the fifth?_____

4. What is the seventh?_____

5. What is the fourth?_____

6. What is the second?_____

7. What is the sixth?_____

8. What is the key signature for G♭ major?_____

Play the 1-3-5-7 in every octave on your instrument.

Step 10: Review G♭ major.

LESSON 15 – C♭ MAJOR SCALE

Step 1: Formula

Step 2: Write the C♭ major scale below.

Step 3: What is the key signature? _____

Step 4: Play it.

Step 5: Listen to it.

Step 6: Analyze it.

Step 7: Verbalize it.

Step 8: Memorize it.

Step 9:

QUIZ 15

1. What is the first degree of C♭ major? _____ *Find them all.*

2. What is the third?_____

3. What is the fifth?_____

4. What is the seventh?_____

5. What is the fourth?_____

6. What is the second?_____

7. What is the sixth?_____

8. What is the key signature for C♭ major?_____

Play the 1-3-5-7 in every octave on your instrument.

Step 10: Review C♭ major.

Congratulations! You've completed all the flat keys.

THE CIRCLE OF FOURTHS

As noted earlier, flat keys move in a **Circle of Fourths**. When moving through the flat keys, the next key is a fourth up, the new accidental is always the fourth, and we keep all previous accidentals when moving to the new key. It works like this:

F major (B♭)

B♭ major (B♭, E♭)

E♭ major (B♭, E♭, A♭)

A♭ major (B♭, E♭, A♭, D♭)

D♭ major (B♭, E♭, A♭, D♭, G♭)

G♭ major (B♭, E♭, A♭, D♭, G♭, C♭)

C♭ major (B♭, E♭, A♭, D♭, G♭, C♭, F♭)

Remember that, enharmonically, C♭ is played like B and F♭ is played like E, but they must be named according to how they occur in the key.

Let's look at a visual representation of the **Circle of Fifths** (sharp keys) and **Circle of Fourths** (flat keys), their corresponding key signatures, and the associated major and minor keys. This will reinforce what we've studied already, and will help pave the way to our discussion of **related keys**, which follows.

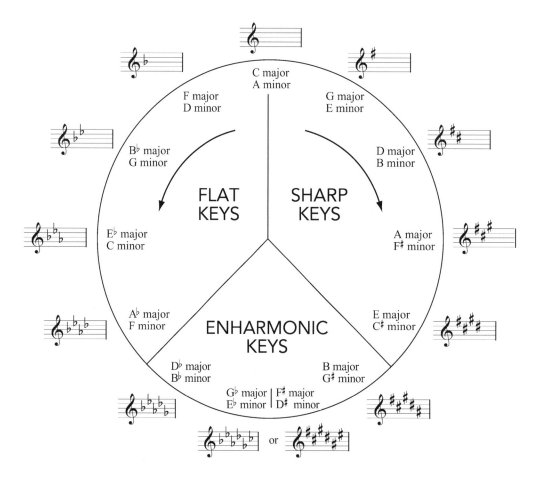

Beginning at the top of the circle with C major/A minor, we move to the right along the Circle of Fifths and the sharp keys. Starting from the same point and moving left, we follow the Circle of Fourths and the flat keys. At the bottom of the circle, there are several intersecting **enharmonic keys**.

ENHARMONIC KEYS

As mentioned earlier, the term **enharmonic** is used to indicate different ways of spelling the same note: for example, D♯ = E♭, G♭ = F♯, E♯ = F♮, etc. Likewise, keys themselves may be considered enharmonic keys.

For the sake of comprehensiveness, we are learning to spell *all* the keys, but be aware that, from a practical standpoint, it is unusual to encounter the keys C♯ major/A♯ minor and C♭ major/A♭ minor. Rather, we more often find D♭ major/B minor and B major/G♯ minor.

You may wish to review all major scales at this point. If you really know them, working one key at a time, you should be able to:

- Play the major scale.
- Play the 1-3-5-7.
- Know the key signature.
- Know all degrees.

Can you do this for all these keys?

C	G	D	A	E	B	F♯	C♯
F	B♭	E♭	A♭	D♭	G♭	C♭	

So, what good is all this study on major scales? You ask, "What will it do for me?" Major scales provide melody, bass parts, string parts, etc. One of the biggest uses is that, when harmonized, the scales tell us the most common and predictable chords used in progressions in most songs today. This is a big deal! When we begin to study chords, chords in keys, and chord substitutions, you will see why scale study is so important.

INTRODUCTION TO MINOR SCALES

For each major key, there are three related **minor scales**. We will explain and explore as we go. First, some terminology.

Tonal center: the apparent home of tonality for the ear. It usually is the first note/chord and last note/chord sounded in a scale, progression, or song.

Relative keys: major and minor scales that have the same key signatures. The relative minor begins on the sixth scale degree of the relative major and shares the same key signature. For example, C major is the relative major of A minor, E minor is the relative minor of G major. Relative keys do not share the same **tonal center**.

Accidental: a sign placed in front of a note to change its previous pitch.

> **sharp** (♯): raises a note by a half step
>
> **double sharp** (𝄪): raises a note by a whole step
>
> **flat** (♭): lowers a note by a half step
>
> **double flat** (♭♭): lowers a note by a whole step
>
> **natural** (♮): cancels a previous sharp or flat

Double sharps and double flats often produce enharmonic spellings. For example, F𝄪 = G, A♭♭ = G, etc.

As we move into the following lessons, you will want to memorize these three formulas:

> **1. Natural (or relative) minor scale:** contains only the notes in the the major key signature
>
> **2. Harmonic minor:** the seventh note is raised a half step both ascending and descending
>
> **3. Melodic minor:** the sixth and seventh notes are raised when ascending, then returned to the natural minor when descending

MINOR SCALES
THE SHARP KEYS

LESSON 16 — A MINOR SCALES

Let's begin by looking at the C major scale below.

No sharps and no flats, right? Look at the sixth degree, A. This note is the tonal center for the minor scales to follow. Therefore, C is the "relative major" and A is the "relative minor." **The formula: To find the relative minor of a major scale, go to the sixth note/degree of the major scale.**

But what if you have only the relative minor note to start from? How then do you find the relative major and its key signature? That's easy: From the tonal center (A), go up a minor third (1½ steps). **The formula: To find the relative major of a minor scale, go to the third note/degree of the minor scale.**

Refer to the chart on page 22. Take some time to get this straight. It is important that you understand this concept. Memorize everything up to this point.

Now let's construct the first minor scale, the **natural minor**.

Natural Minor

The sixth of C major is A. This becomes the first note and the tonal center in the new scale. We go up one octave to A and descend downward to A, using the same key signature as C major.

For now, we will number the notes 1–8 ascending and reverse order descending. Again, notes A to A, no sharps and no flats, same key signature and same notes as the relative major, but the **tonal center** has switched from C to A.

Play the natural minor scale a few times ascending and descending. Then play C major a few times ascending and descending. See what we mean by the tonal center seeming to change from the A to the C. Okay, so we have the natural minor. Let's look at a second type of minor scale, the **harmonic minor**.

Harmonic Minor

Step 1: Formula. Starting on A, the seventh note is raised a half step both ascending and descending.

Play the scale a few times. Notice the #7 makes it sound like Middle Eastern, snake-charmer music. That is a very distinctive characteristic of this scale. Whenever you hear that sound, you know it's the harmonic minor.

The third type of minor scale is the **melodic minor**.

Melodic Minor

Step 1: Formula. The sixth and seventh are raised a half step ascending, and returned to the natural minor descending.

Play the scale a few times. The first four notes look like the natural minor scale, and the last four take on the characteristics of a major scale, descending like the natural minor.

Step 2: Now write all three scales for the key of A minor. Be sure to write ascending and descending.

Step 3: The key signature is same as C major, no sharps and no flats.

Step 3: The key signature is the same, but with one accidental, G♯.

A harmonic minor

Step 3: The key signature is the same, but with two accidentals (F♯ and G♯) ascending, then back to natural minor descending.

A melodic minor

Step 4: Play all the scales again.

Step 5: Listen to them. Record them. Be able to identify them by listening.

Step 6: Analyze.

Step 7: Verbalize.

Step 8: Memorize.

If you have trouble remembering the formula for the harmonic and melodic minors and which one sharps what, try this tip: H comes before M in the alphabet, and the number one comes before the number two. So the harmonic minor scale has one extra accidental sharp, while the melodic has two. Any word or number type association you can apply to help remember things is okay. Just do it!

Step 9:

QUIZ 16

1. What key is the relative major to A minor? _____

2. What is the formula for the natural minor scale?_____

_____

3. What is the formula for the harmonic minor scale? _____

_____

4. What is the formula for the melodic minor scale? _____

_____

5. Define and give an example of "tonal center." _____

_____

Step 10: Review.

Now would be a good time to stop and review all that has been discussed so far regarding the minor scales.

LESSON 17 — E MINOR SCALES

The first task here is to determine the relative major scale. If E is the tonal center, a minor third up must be _____. Right: G major! And the key signature it will share is _____. Right: F♯.

Write the three scales for E minor below, ascending and descending.

E natural minor (formula?)

E harmonic minor (formula?)

E melodic minor (formula?)

Step 3: Key Signatures

- The E natural minor scale has the second note as an F♯, all others natural.
- The E harmonic minor scale has the second note (F♯) and the seventh note (D♯) sharped.
- The E melodic minor scale has the second (F♯), sixth (C♯), and seventh (D♯) sharped when ascending and D♮ and C♮ when descending. Did you get these?

Step 4: Play.

Step 5: Listen.

Step 6: Analyze.

Step 7: Verbalize.

Step 8: Memorize.

Step 9:

QUIZ 17

1. What is the relative minor for G major? _____

2. What is the second note in the E natural minor scale? _____

3. What is the seventh note in the E harmonic scale? _____

4. What is the sixth note in the E melodic minor scale? _____

5. What is the seventh note in the E melodic minor scale? _____

Step 10: Review.

LESSON 18 — B MINOR SCALES

The relative major for B minor is D major. Its key signature is two sharps, F♯ and C♯. Write the three minor scales below, ascending and descending.

B natural minor (formula?)

B harmonic minor (formula?)

B melodic minor (formula?)

Step 3: Key Signatures

- The natural minor has C♯ as the second note, F♯ as the fifth note.
- The harmonic minor has the same, plus the seventh as A♯.
- The melodic minor has the C♯, F♯, G♯ (sixth), and A♯ (seventh) ascending, with A♮ and G♮ descending.

This is the last help of this type. For a summary of the sharp-key minor scales, see the quiz after Lesson 23 (page 36).

Step 4: Play all three minor scales in as many octaves as you can.

Step 5: Listen.

Step 6: Analyze.

Step 7: Verbalize.

Step 8: Memorize.

Step 9:

QUIZ 18

1. What is the key signature for the minor scales related to D major? _____
2. What are the sharped notes in the natural minor scale? _____
3. What are the sharped notes in the harmonic minor scale? _____
4. What are the sharped notes in the melodic minor scale?_____

Step 10: Review.

LESSON 19 — F♯ MINOR SCALES

What is the relative major for F♯ minor? _____

What is its key signature? _____

Write the three minor scales below, ascending and descending.

natural minor (formula?)

harmonic minor (formula?)

melodic minor (formula?)

Step 3: Do you know all three key signatures and accidentals?

Step 4: Play all three minor scales in as many octaves as you can.

Step 5: Listen.

Step 6: Analyze.

Step 7: Verbalize.

Step 8: Memorize.

Step 9:

QUIZ 19

1. What is the key signature for the relative major scale? _____

2. What are the sharped notes in the natural minor scale? _____

3. What are the sharped notes in the harmonic minor scale? _____

4. What are the sharped notes in the melodic minor scale? _____

Step 10: Review.

LESSON 20 — C♯ MINOR SCALES

Determine the relative major scale and write the three minor scales below, ascending and descending.

Step 3: Do you know all the key signatures and accidentals for the sharp minor scales?

Step 4: Play all three minor scales in as many octaves as you can.

Step 5: Listen.

Step 6: Analyze.

Step 7: Verbalize.

Step 8: Memorize.

Step 9:

QUIZ 20

1. What is the relative major key? _____

2. What are the sharped notes in the relative minor scale?_____

3. What are the sharped notes in the harmonic minor scale? _____

4. What are the sharped notes in the melodic minor scale?

_____

Step 10: Review.

LESSON 21 — G♯ MINOR SCALES

Determine the relative major scale and write the three minor scales below, ascending and descending.

When a note must be a double sharp because of the scale rules, it is notated as ✖ in front of the note. Be careful in the harmonic and melodic minor scales below. From now on, all sharp-key minor scales will have some double sharps.

Step 3: Do you know all the key signatures and accidentals?

Step 4: Play all three minor scales in as many octaves as you can.

Step 5: Listen.

Step 6: Analyze.

Step 7: Verbalize.

Step 8: Memorize.

Step 9:

QUIZ 21

1. What is the relative major key? _____

2. What are the sharped notes in the relative minor scale?_____

3. What are the sharped notes in the harmonic minor scale? _____

4. What are the sharped notes in the melodic minor scale? _____

Step 10: Review.

LESSON 22 — D♯ MINOR SCALES

Determine the relative major scale and write the three minor scales below, ascending and descending.

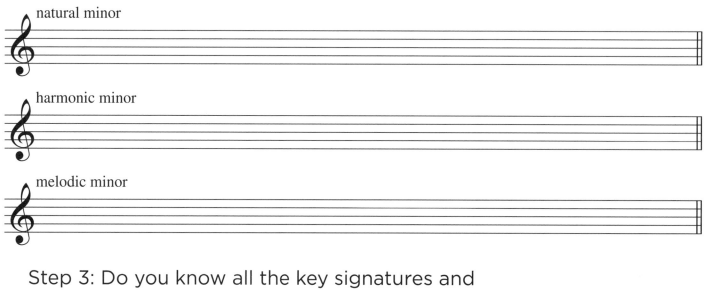

natural minor

harmonic minor

melodic minor

Step 3: Do you know all the key signatures and accidentals?

Step 4: Play all three minor scales in as many octaves as you can.

Step 5: Listen.

Step 6: Analyze.

Step 7: Verbalize.

Step 8: Memorize.

Step 9:

QUIZ 22

1. What is the relative major key? _____

2. What are the sharped notes in the relative minor scale?_____

3. What are the sharped notes in the harmonic minor scale? _____

4. What are the sharped notes in the melodic minor scale? _____

Step 10: Review.

LESSON 23 — A♯ MINOR SCALES

Determine the relative major scale and write the three minor scales below, ascending and descending.

natural minor

harmonic minor

melodic minor

Step 3: Do you know all the key signatures and accidentals?

Step 4: Play all three minor scales in as many octaves as you can.

Step 5: Listen.

Step 6: Analyze.

Step 7: Verbalize.

Step 8: Memorize.

Step 9:

QUIZ 23

1. What is the relative major key for A♯ minor? _____

2. What are the sharped notes in the natural minor scale?_____

3. What are the sharped notes in the harmonic minor scale? _____

4. What are the sharped notes in the melodic minor scale?_____

5. In the sharp-keys minor scales, which is the first to use double sharps? _____

6. What is the relative minor of C major? _____

7. What is the relative minor of G major? _____

8. What is the relative minor of D major? _____

9. What is the relative minor of A major? _____

10. What is the relative minor of E major? _____

11. What is the relative minor of B major? _____

12. What is the relative minor of F♯ major? _____

13. What is the relative minor of C♯ major? _____

Step 10: Review.

For a complete listing of all the sharp-key minor scales, see the Answer Section, beginning on page 100.

SECTION D

MINOR SCALES
THE FLAT KEYS

LESSON 24 — D MINOR SCALES

Determine the relative major key and write the three minor scales below, ascending and descending.

natural minor

harmonic minor

melodic minor

Step 3: Do you know the key signatures and the accidentals used in all three minor scales?

Step 4: Play.

Step 5: Listen.

Step 6: Analyze.

Step 7: Verbalize.

Step 8: Memorize.

Step 9:

QUIZ 24

1. What is the relative major key? _____

2. What is its key signature? _____

3. What are the sharp notes in the natural minor scale? _____

4. What are the sharp notes in the harmonic minor scale? _____

5. What are the sharp notes in the melodic minor scale? _____

Step 10: Review.

LESSON 25 — G MINOR SCALES

Determine the relative major key and write the three minor scales below, ascending and descending.

natural minor

harmonic minor

melodic minor

Step 3: Do you know the key signatures and the accidentals used in all three minor scales?

Step 4: Play.

Step 5: Listen.

Step 6: Analyze.

Step 7: Verbalize.

Step 8: Memorize.

Step 9:

QUIZ 25

1. What is the relative major key? _____

2. What are the sharp notes in the natural minor scale?_____

3. What are the sharp notes in the harmonic minor scale?_____

4. What are the sharp notes in the melodic minor scale? _____

5. What other notes are different than you might expect in the melodic minor scale? (hint: the sixth)_____

Step 10: Review.

LESSON 26 — C MINOR SCALES

Determine the relative major key and write the three minor scales below, ascending and descending.

natural minor

harmonic minor

melodic minor

Step 3: Do you know the relative major key signature and the three minor scale accidentals?

Step 4: Play.

Step 5: Listen.

Step 6: Analyze.

Step 7: Verbalize.

Step 8: Memorize.

Step 9:

QUIZ 26

1. What is the relative major key? _____

2. What are the new sharp notes or natural notes in the natural minor scale?

   _____

3. What are the new sharp notes or natural notes in the harmonic minor scale?

   _____

4. What are the new sharp notes or natural notes in the melodic minor scale?

   _____

Step 10: Review.

LESSON 27 — F MINOR SCALES

Determine the relative major key and write the three minor scales below, ascending and descending.

natural minor

harmonic minor

melodic minor

Step 3: Do you know the relative major key signature and the accidentals introduced in the minor scale?

Step 4: Play.

Step 5: Listen.

Step 6: Analyze.

Step 7: Verbalize.

Step 8: Memorize.

Step 9:

QUIZ 27

1. What is the relative major key and key signature? _____

2. What are the new accidentals introduced in the relative minor scale?

_____

3. What are the new accidentals introduced in the harmonic minor scale?

_____

4. What are the new accidentals introduced in the melodic minor scale?

_____

Step 10: Review.

LESSON 28 — B♭ MINOR SCALES

Determine the relative major key and write the three minor scales below, ascending and descending.

natural minor

harmonic minor

melodic minor

Step 3: Do you know the relative major key signature and the accidentals used in the three minor scales?

Step 4: Play.

Step 5: Listen.

Step 6: Analyze.

Step 7: Verbalize.

Step 8: Memorize.

Step 9:

QUIZ 28

1. What is the relative major key and key signature? _____

2. What are the new accidentals introduced in the natural minor scale?

   _____

3. What are the new accidentals introduced in the harmonic minor scale?

   _____

4. What are the new accidentals introduced in the melodic minor scale?

   _____

Step 10: Review.

LESSON 29 — E♭ MINOR SCALES

Determine the relative major key and write the three minor scales below, ascending and descending.

Step 3: Do you know the relative major key signature and the accidentals introduced in the three minor scales?

Step 4: Play.

Step 5: Listen.

Step 6: Analyze.

Step 7: Verbalize.

Step 8: Memorize.

Step 9:

QUIZ 29

1. What is the relative major key and key signature, and the accidentals introduced in this set of scales?_____

2. What are the new accidentals introduced in the natural minor scale?

   _____

3. What are the new accidentals introduced in the harmonic minor scale?

   _____

4. What are the new accidentals introduced in the melodic minor scale?

   _____

Step 10: Review.

LESSON 30 — A♭ MINOR SCALES

Determine the relative major key and write the three minor scales below, ascending and descending.

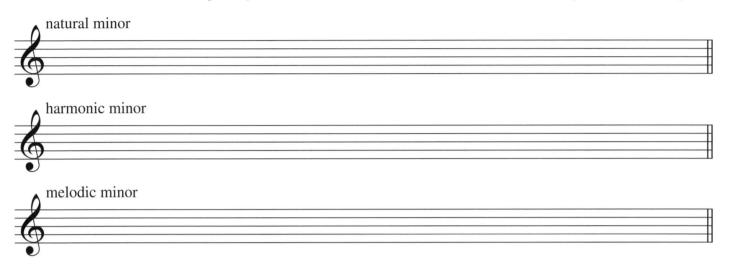

natural minor

harmonic minor

melodic minor

Step 3: Do you know the relative major key signature and the new accidentals introduced in the three minor scales?

Step 4: Play.

Step 5: Listen.

Step 6: Analyze.

Step 7: Verbalize.

Step 8: Memorize.

Step 9:

QUIZ 30

1. What is the relative major key, key signature, and the accidentals introduced in this set of scales? _____

2. What are the new accidentals in the natural minor?

_____

3. What are the new accidentals in the harmonic minor?

_____

4. What are the new accidentals in the melodic minor?

_____

Step 10: Review.

OTHER SCALES

The major and natural minor scales are **diatonic** scales. That is, they divide the octave into five whole steps and two half steps. There are many other scales, modes, etc. that classical music composers have used to create unique effects in writing their music. Avant-garde jazz musicians have used them as well. It is beyond the scope of this workbook to include those here, but we will include several others.

Major Pentatonic Scale

The most common non-diatonic scales in use in today's popular, country, and blues are the major pentatonic scale and the minor pentatonic scale. As you might infer from its name, a *pentatonic scale* contains five notes. The major pentatonic scale is comprised of the first, second, third, fifth, and sixth notes of the major scale. It is found in the music of many Asian peoples, including China and Japan, as well as some African music and European folk music. In the United States, you'll hear its distinctive coloring in folk music, hymns, and spirituals, and pop/rock music – for example, in Led Zeppelin's "Whole Lotta Love.".

For the **C major pentatonic scale**, the sequence is C-D-E-G-A. The example above shows the duplication of the starting note, an octave higher.

This sequence strongly suggests a major sixth chord, and works well with the diatonic I–IV–V progressions we'll see later in this book.

Write and play examples in these keys:

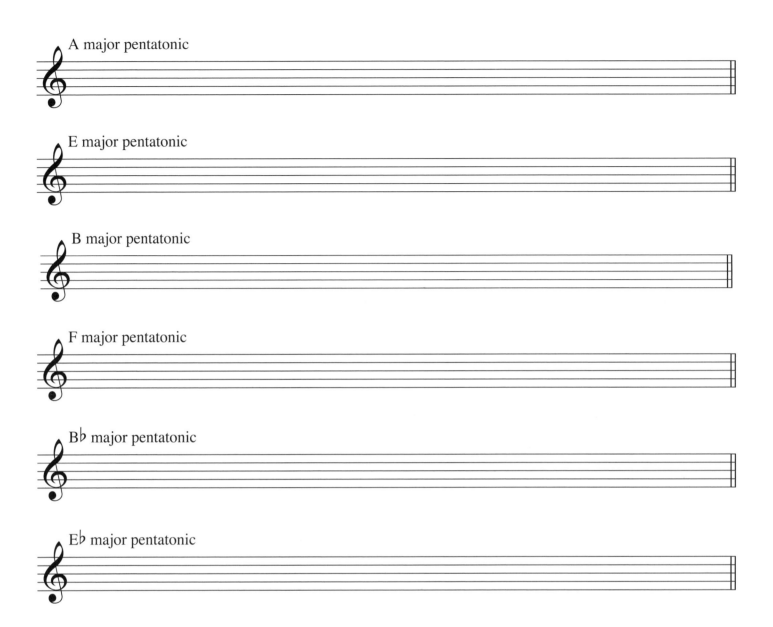

A major pentatonic

E major pentatonic

B major pentatonic

F major pentatonic

B♭ major pentatonic

E♭ major pentatonic

Play. Listen. Analyze. Verbalize. Memorize. Quiz yourself. Review all.

Minor Pentatonic Scale

The minor pentatonic scale is made from the first, third, fourth, fifth, and seventh notes of the natural minor scale. Thus, the sequence for the **C minor pentatonic scale** is C-E♭-F-G-B♭. It is used in a lot of blues music. Again, the example concludes with the starting note, an octave higher.

C minor pentatonic

Eric Clapton likes to use this scale in connection with major or minor chords, since it works well on either dominant seventh progressions or minor seventh chords. Most rock guitarists play this scale using various passing tones and accidentals, delicately weaving in and out of the minor pentatonic pattern.

Write and play the minor pentatonic in the following keys:

Play. Listen. Analyze. Verbalize. Memorize. Quiz yourself. Review all.

Modes

Like the major and natural minor scales, modes are **diatonic** scales. That is, they divide the octave into five whole steps and two half steps. The Ionian mode, for example, starts on C and uses the same pattern as the C major scale; half steps occur in the same places.

Modes can be transposed to any tonal center, but to find their initial formulas, start on a white key on the keyboard and play eight notes to the octave.

Here, for example, is the Dorian mode:

Dorian scale (mode)

A to A: Aeolian mode (same as the natural minor scale)

B to B: Locrian mode

C to C: Ionian mode (same as the major scale)

D to D: Dorian mode

E to E: Phrygian mode

F to F: Lydian mode

G to G: Mixolydian mode

You can experiment with other modes as you like. Search in the library or online for a more complete discussion.

Hungarian Minor Scale

For a real gypsy type sound, try the **Hungarian minor scale**. Transpose it to other keys as you like.

Hungarian minor scale

Whole Tone Scale

The **whole tone scale** is comprised entirely of whole steps. Notice that there are only seven notes in the scale. It was favored by the Impressionist composer Claude Debussy, and Stevie Wonder used it in the intro to "You Are the Sunshine of My Life."

whole tone scale

Chromatic Scales

Chromatic scales move exclusively in half steps, and can be used in all types of music. Below is an ascending (using sharps) and descending (using flats) chromatic octave. You can start and end at any point, depending on the key.

Diminished Scales

The half diminished scale is used with half diminished chords.

The fully diminished scale is used with fully diminished chords.

Notice that the fully diminished scale comprised entirely of minor thirds (m3). This is the most common type of diminished scale.

As mentioned earlier, there are many scales, modes, etc. that are not in this book. If they pique your interest, consult your public library or search online for more information. Be sure to transpose all of the above into other keys.

PART TWO
HARMONY, INTERVALS & CHORD STRUCTURE

CHORDS BY DEGREE

Now that you have scale theory to draw from, we will fill in some gaps and answer some questions that you have been asking yourself. As in Part One, all examples are to be played, listened to, analyzed, and memorized before going to the next key or example. I realize that this can be burdensome, but believe me, if this is going to be a tool to use at your slightest whim in the creative process, you **must** learn it this way.

First, some simple definitions:

Interval: the distance from one note to another, expressed in steps and labeled by a specific name or type of interval; example: two steps = major third (M3)

Harmony: at least two notes sounded together; there could be three, four, five, or more notes as well

Chord: at least three notes sounded together; there could be four notes (seventh chords), five notes (ninth chords), or six notes (11th chords), or more

Triad: a three-note chord

In Section A, we will explore in the simplest approach to learning chord structure – by degree. Here you will find:

- major chords
- minor chords
- augmented chords
- diminished chords
- major seventh chords
- dominant seventh chords
- minor seventh chords
- minor/major seventh chords
- half diminished seventh chords
- fully diminished seventh chords
- augmented seventh chords
- major sixth chords
- minor sixth chords
- major ninth chords
- dominant ninth chords
- minor ninth chords
- suspended chords
- major 11th chords
- dominant 11th chords
- major 13th chords
- dominant 13th chords
- extended and altered chords
- and more

Section B will deal with the same chords, but using the interval method. To maximize information, you will need to memorize both the chord-by-degree and chord-by-interval approaches. The answers always come out the same, but each can be used in different situations.

The first method of chord structure – by degree – is best for sheer recall. The second method – by interval – is useful in improvising and transposing parts.

Later on, in Section C, we will look at examples of progressions and substitutions of chords.

MAJOR TRIADS

To construct a major chord in any key, take the scale and play the first, third, and fifth degrees together. Don't forget the key signature!

First, write the C major scale.

C major scale

Now let's write the first, third, fifth degrees together, like this:

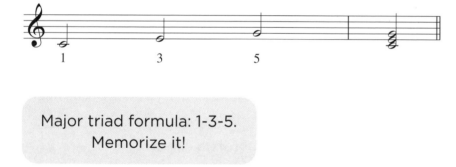

1   3   5

> Major triad formula: 1-3-5.
> Memorize it!

This is a **root position chord**. In other words, the chord is played in the order of 1-3-5, C-E-G. We could write and play those notes in any order, such as the first inversion or the second inversion below. Any way you play C-E-G in any combination, as many Cs, Es, or Gs as you want – in as many octaves as you want – the answer is still the same. In the key of C major, C-E-G (1-3-5) in any combination is a **C major chord**. Got it?

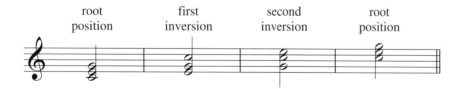

root position   first inversion   second inversion   root position

These three notes might be played on the same instrument (like the piano or guitar), they might be sung by three singers or a whole choir as vocal harmonies, or they might be played separately by different instruments. In any event, they spell the same chord.

From now on in our studies, we will use the root position chords to learn our keys. After you improve, you can use the other inversions.

All examples will begin in C. You will need to duplicate this in all other keys to complete the assignment. Write the following major triads below:

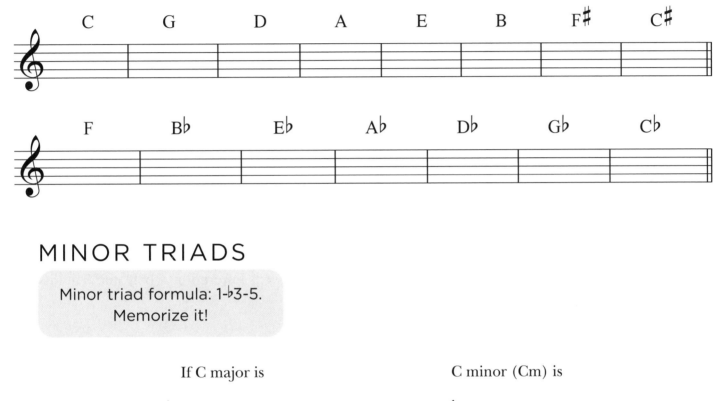

MINOR TRIADS

Minor triad formula: 1-♭3-5.
Memorize it!

If C major is | then | C minor (Cm) is

C = C-E-G | C minor = C-E♭-G

It's that easy. Take the major chord and lower the third degree by a half step to E♭. Now write each chord above next to the example.

The C major scale gives us no sharps and no flats in its true diatonic state, but composers can alter the scales or chords with accidentals at any time to provide mood. Is this okay? Certainly. Just recognize these as accidentals inserted into the piece. We will also discover that all the chords discussed in this section will be used not only in C, but in other keys as well. So don't let accidentals confuse you. Just memorize these formulas and chord structures for now. More explanation will follow.

Write the following minor triads below:

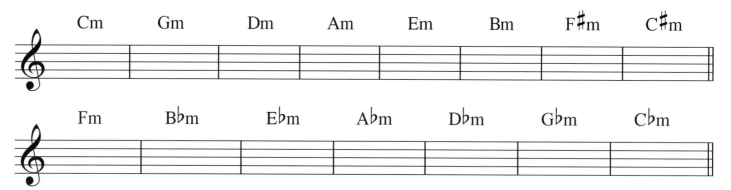

DIMINISHED TRIADS

Diminished triad formula: 1-♭3-♭5.
Memorize it!

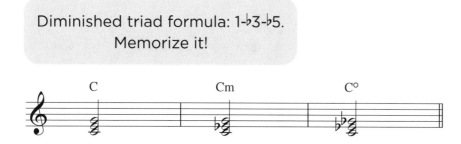

The chord on the right is C diminished. It can be written C° or C dim. "Diminished" means the pitch is lowered by a half step. In this case, the fifth degree is lowered by a half step from its position in the minor chord.

N.B. "…from its position in the minor chord." If only the fifth degree in the major chord is flatted, you get C-E-G♭. That gives you a different chord, the C(♭5).

For a diminished triad, you must have the ♭3 and the ♭5. Write the following diminished chords below.

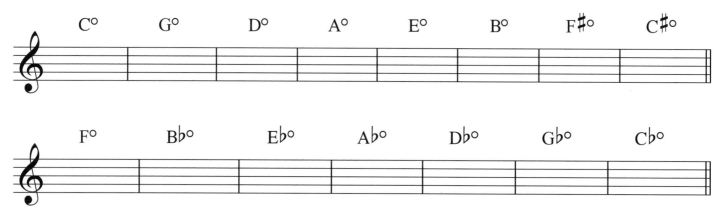

AUGMENTED TRIADS

Augmented triad formula: 1-3-#5.
Memorize it!

The plus sign (+) is another way of designating the augmented chord. "Augmented" means the pitch is raised a half step. In this, case it means to raise the fifth degree by a half step. Write the following chords below.

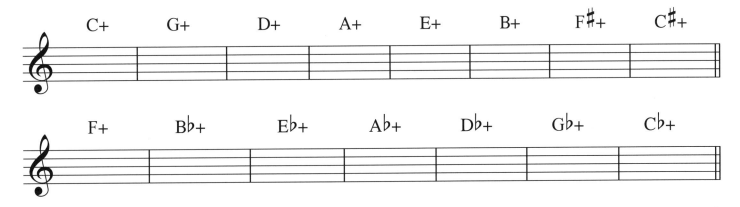

Major. Minor. Diminished. Augmented. These four represent the basic structure for all chords. Everything hereafter will begin with one of these four basic triad structures. Note that in some sharp keys, the fifth degree of augmented triads is a double sharp (×). For example, C#+=C#-E#-G×.

Write the following augmented (+) chords below.

Now, working one key at a time, review all the chord structures covered so far. Recite them verbally until you have memorized each one. This is a lot of work, but it will make everything from here on much easier. Don't try to memorize all of this in one day or one week. You may not get it. Go slowly and absorb it. If it takes you a week to learn two or three keys, so what? Once you get it, you own it!

Example: C is C-E-G   Cm is C-E♭-G   C° is C-E♭-G♭   C+ is C-E-G♯

Make sure you have the formulas memorized also.

You now have 60 basic chords: 15 keys x 4 chords = 60 chords.

SEVENTH CHORDS

Major seventh chord formula: 1-3-5-7.
Memorize it!

Example: C major 7 or Cmaj7. The latter is preferred.

Cmaj7 = C-E-G-B.

Notice that now we are dealing with four-note chords. The major seventh chord is constructed by taking the major triad and adding the seventh degree as it occurs in the key signature.

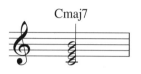

Write the following major seventh chords below.

Cmaj7   Gmaj7   Dmaj7   Amaj7   Emaj7   Bmaj7   F♯maj7   C♯maj7

Fmaj7   B♭maj7   E♭maj7   A♭maj7   D♭maj7   G♭maj7   C♭maj7

Dominant seventh chord formula: 1-3-5-♭7.
Memorize it!

So, C7 = C-E-G-B♭. From this point on, unless the chord specifies "major 7" it is understood that the seventh degree is to be flatted.

Write the following chords below.

Minor seventh chord formula: 1-♭3-5-♭7.
Memorize it!

Example: C minor 7 or Cm7. The minor seventh chord is constructed by taking the minor triad and adding the lowered (by a half step) seventh degree. So, a Cm7 = C-E♭-G-B♭.

Be careful with the Gm7, and in other similar situations. The structure of the Gm7 is G-B♭-D-F. The seventh of G is F♯, so if you flat (lower) a sharped note, it becomes a natural note.

Write the following minor seventh chords below.

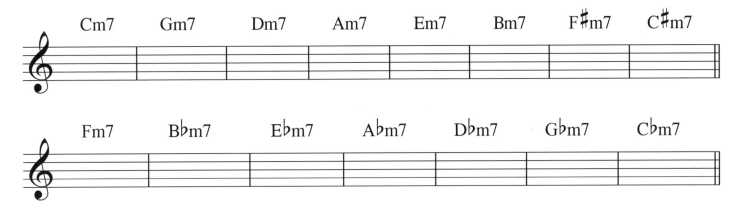

57

Minor/major seventh chord formula: 1-♭3-5-7.

The best way to distinguish this chord is min/maj7 or m(maj7). It's the second chord in Led Zeppelin's "Stairway to Heaven." It is used in George Benson's "Masquerade" and a lot of other songs. It will sound dissonant when used by itself, but when played in the progression of minor, min/maj seventh, then minor seventh, you will see how it fits. This chord is almost always used this way, hardly ever as a stand-alone chord.

Cm(maj7) = C-E♭-G-B

Write the following chords below.

Cm(maj7) Gm(maj7) Dm(maj7) Am(maj7) Em(maj7) Bm(maj7) F♯m(maj7) C♯m(maj7)

Fm(maj7) B♭m(maj7) E♭m(maj7) A♭m(maj7) D♭m(maj7) G♭m(maj7) C♭m(maj7)

DIMINISHED SEVENTH CHORDS

There are two types of diminished chords: the half diminished seventh (∅), and the fully diminished seventh (○).

Half diminished seventh chord formula: 1-♭3-♭5-♭7.
Fully diminished seventh chord formula: 1-♭3-♭5-♭♭7.

Yes, a double-flatted seventh: C-E♭-G♭-B♭♭. Note that the ♭♭7 looks and sounds like the sixth degree, but is not! It must be called by the name of the seventh degree. (Later in this section, there will be more explanations on intervals and chords by intervals.) See below.

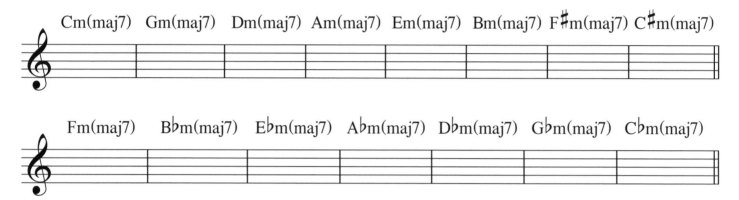

Write the half diminished and fully diminished seventh chords below, side by side.

C∅7   C○7   G∅7   G○7   D∅7   D○7   A∅7   A○7

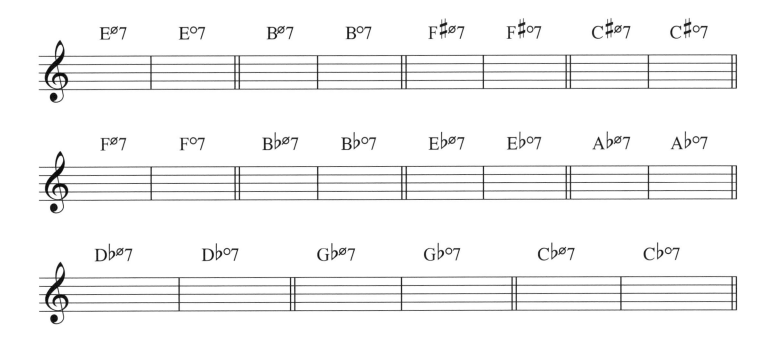

AUGMENTED SEVENTH CHORDS

Augmented (+) seventh chord formula: 1-3-♯5-♭7.

The augmented seventh chord is noted like this: C+7. But please note that it is the fifth that is raised, not the seventh! C+7 = C-E-G♯-B♭

Write the following chords below.

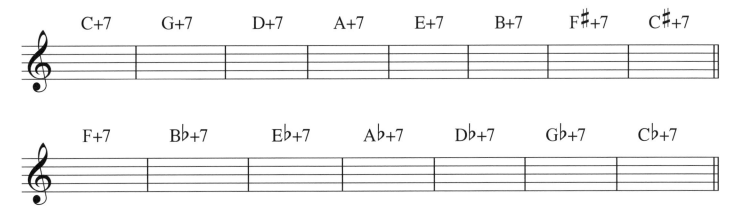

Both in fully diminished and augmented (+) chords, any note in the chord may be used as the root. This has to do with the 12 half steps in the diatonic octave and the relationship of four notes versus three notes and a repeating pattern in both chords.

SIXTH CHORDS

Major sixth chord formula: 1-3-5-6.

Just a plain sixth chord, such as C6 is okay. Some older sheet music or books may insist on using "major sixth." C6 = C-E-G-A

Write the following chords below.

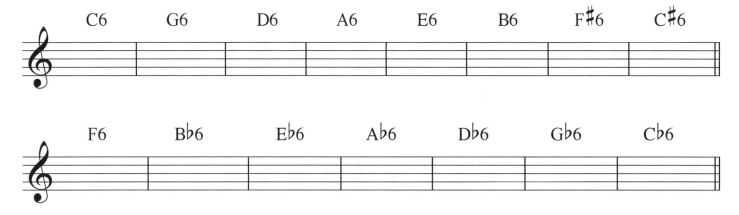

Minor sixth chord formula: 1-♭3-5-6.

Write the following minor sixth chords below.

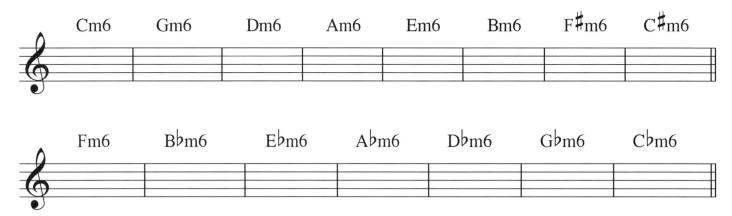

Note: When dealing with chords that have four or more notes, the name of the chord is often determined by how the chord is used, what key is being used, and what chords precede and follow the chord in question. We'll touch on this in more detail when we get to Chord Progressions and Substitutions.

NINTH CHORDS

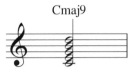

Major ninth chord formula: 1-3-5-7-9.
C major 9 or Cmaj9 = C-E-G-B-D

Remember, the ninth degree is the same as the second degree up one octave. Also note that this is our first five-note chord.

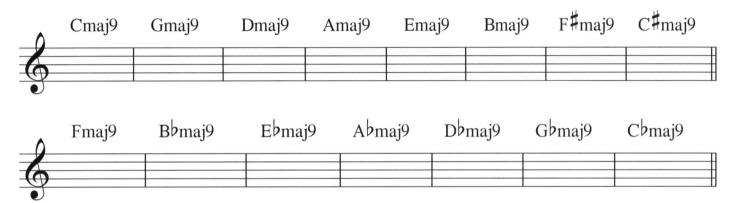

Write the following major ninth chords below.

Cmaj9   Gmaj9   Dmaj9   Amaj9   Emaj9   Bmaj9   F♯maj9   C♯maj9

Fmaj9   B♭maj9   E♭maj9   A♭maj9   D♭maj9   G♭maj9   C♭maj9

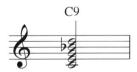

Dominant ninth chord formula: 1-3-5-♭7-9.
C9 = C-E-G-B♭-D

C9 means add the ♭7 to the chord. On the other hand, the term "C major 9" is used to indicate that the seventh is not flatted. So, from now on, any chord that is designated as major 9, major 11, major 13, etc., has the seventh, as is in the key. A 9th, 11th, or 13th chord is understood to have the ♭7.

Write the following dominant ninth chords below.

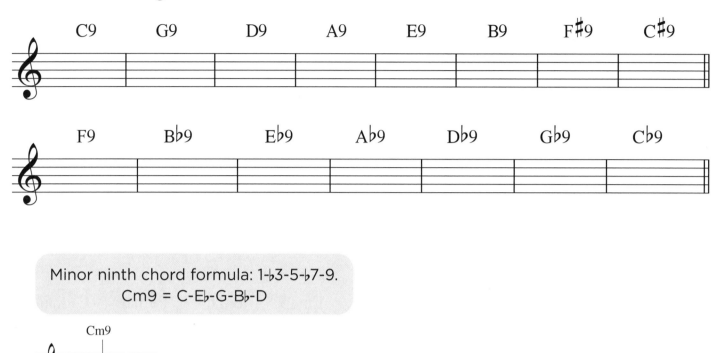

Minor ninth chord formula: 1-♭3-5-♭7-9.
Cm9 = C-E♭-G-B♭-D

Write the following minor ninth chords below.

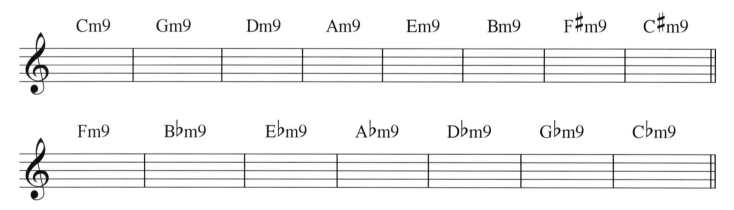

SUSPENDED CHORDS

Usually, a suspended chord means the fourth degree is inserted into the triad in place of the third degree for a momentary transition, hence the term "suspended." The chord will resolve (move down) to the associated major or minor chord, thus ending the tension created by the suspended note. In sheet music, you may see these labeled as Csus4 or, more commonly, Csus. It is understood that the fourth degree is suspended. In this example, Csus (C-F-G) resolves to C major (C-E-G).

Play these. They are very common. You've heard them thousands of times.

There can be also be a suspended second (shown above), suspended ninth, etc. Whatever the suspension, by its very nature, it should resolve to the associated chord. If it does not resolve, it probably should be called by another name, and if so, usually has more than three notes.

11th CHORDS

Major 11th chord formula: 1-3-5-7-9-11.
C major 11 or Cmaj11 = C-E-G-B-D-F

Remember: The 11th degree is the same as the fourth degree up one octave. Also, we have our first six-note chord.

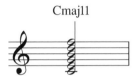

Write the following major 11th chords.

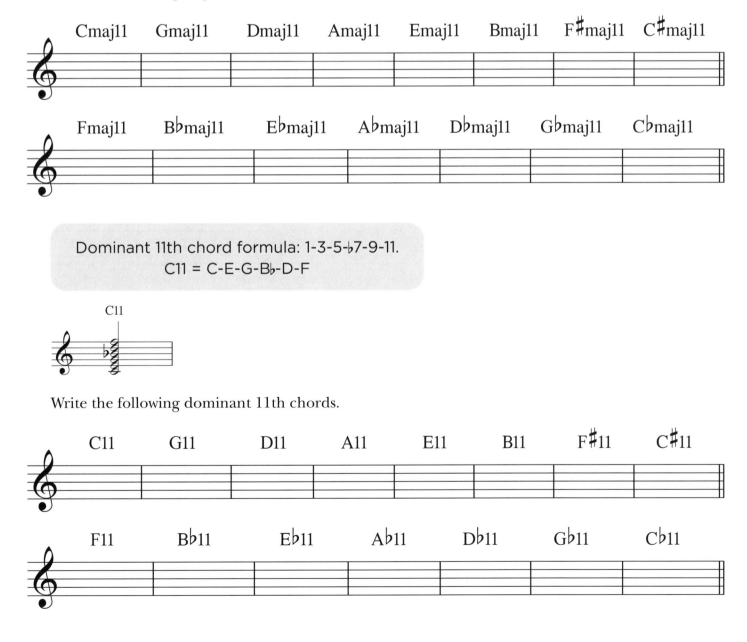

Dominant 11th chord formula: 1-3-5-♭7-9-11.
C11 = C-E-G-B♭-D-F

Write the following dominant 11th chords.

13th CHORDS

There are two types of 13th chords: major and dominant. Most 13th chords will be of the dominant variety. Don't forget that 13 is same as the sixth degree up one octave.

> Major 13th chord formula: 1-3-5-7-9-11-13.
> Cmaj13 = C-E-G-B-D-F-A
>
> Dominant 13th chord formula: 1-3-5-♭7-9-11-13.
> C13 = C-E-G-B♭-D-F-A

This is our first seven-note chord. What are guitar players to do, since they have only six strings? They're going to omit the root (first degree) in the chord. Someone will play it – the keyboard or the bass – or the mind will imagine it anyway.

Write the following major 13th chords and dominant 13th chords.

| Cmaj13 | Gmaj13 | Dmaj13 | Amaj13 | Emaj13 | Bmaj13 | F♯maj13 | C♯maj13 |

| C13 | G13 | D13 | A13 | E13 | B13 | F♯13 | C♯13 |

| Fmaj13 | B♭maj13 | E♭maj13 | A♭maj13 | D♭maj13 | G♭maj13 | C♭maj13 |

| F13 | B♭13 | E♭13 | A♭13 | D♭13 | G♭13 | C♭13 |

EXTENDED AND ALTERED CHORDS

The variations of extended and altered chords are almost endless, but don't let this overwhelm you. As time goes on, they will become easier to understand. You will see:

$$C7\flat9 = 1\text{-}3\text{-}5\text{-}\flat7\text{-}\flat9 \qquad C\text{-}E\text{-}G\text{-}B\flat\text{-}D\flat$$

$$C7\flat5 = 1\text{-}3\text{-}\flat5\text{-}\flat7 \qquad C\text{-}E\text{-}G\flat\text{-}B\flat$$

$$C7\sharp9 = 1\text{-}3\text{-}5\text{-}\flat7\text{-}\sharp9 \qquad C\text{-}E\text{-}G\text{-}B\flat\text{-}D\sharp$$

$$C7\sharp5(\flat9) = 1\text{-}3\text{-}\sharp5\text{-}\flat7\text{-}\flat9 \qquad C\text{-}E\text{-}G\sharp\text{-}B\flat\text{-}D\flat$$

$$C13\flat5(\flat9) = 1\text{-}3\text{-}\flat5\text{-}\flat7\text{-}\flat9\text{-}11\text{-}13 \qquad C\text{-}E\text{-}G\flat\text{-}B\flat\text{-}D\flat\text{-}F\text{-}A$$

Note: Even though C major does not have sharp notes in the scale, you will notice that certain chords contain them. For example, the C7$\sharp$9 has a D$\sharp$. Remember, this is an "altered" chord, and "altered" suggests "not as usual," so it is okay for this to occur. Also note, the pitch should correctly be called D$\sharp$ not E$\flat$, because we sharped the ninth, which is same as second degree but up one octave. Any time we talk of altering the E (the third), we're dealing with the major versus minor chord issue. If you are confused about this, stop now and review.

This is a lot of information, and it may seem hard to digest in this format. Often, the easiest way to learn and remember chords is within the context of the song. However, to learn all of these chords you would need to learn hundreds and hundreds of songs in all styles, which would take years. Take heart! Once you've jumped these hurdles, it gets easier from here on.

The following quiz will be given in a chord progression format that feels more like a song. Any written inversion of the chord is okay, but you may feel more confident in writing the root position chord. All progressions should be played and listened to carefully.

QUIZ

Get a blank sheet of manuscript paper and write the following chords. The first time, use root position triads so that you can apply what you have learned in the last section.

Example 1: root position triads

Get another sheet of manuscript paper and write the chords again. This time, you do not have to keep all chords in root position. Good composition and orchestration usually dictate moving only the notes necessary to move to the next chord.

Example 2: moving to closest note method

Write the chords again, and write them a different way. There can be several variations of the chord progression inversions, but they are still the same chords.

Example 3: moving to closest note (triad) with root tone as bass

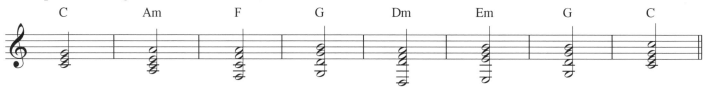

Write these chord progressions three ways on manuscript paper.
- Cmaj7–Am7–Fmaj7–G7–Dm7–Em7–G7–Cmaj7
- C7–F7–G7–C7
- C9–F9–G9–C9
- C–C+–C6–C7–F–Fm–G–G+7–C
- Cmaj7–C6–Cm7–Cm6–Em7–E♭m7–Dm7–G11–Cmaj7
- Dm7–D11–G13–G13♭9–G13♯5♭9–Cmaj7
- C–C♯dim–Dm–D♯dim7–Em–F–F♯dim7–G–G♯dim7–Am7
- C–Csus–C–Csus2–C–F–Fsus–F–Fsus2–F–G–Gsus–G–Gsus2–G–C
- F–Dm–B♭–C–Gm–Am–C–F
- Fmaj7–Dm7–B♭maj7–C7–Gm7–Am7–C7–Fmaj7
- F7–B♭7–C7–F7–F9–B♭9–C9–F9
- F–F+–F6–F7–B♭–B♭m–C–C+7
- Fmaj7–F6–Fm7–Fm6–Am7–Abm7–Gm7–C11–Fmaj7
- FM7–G11–C13–C15♭9–C13♭5♭9–Fmaj7
- F–F♯dim–Gm–G♯dim7–Am7–B♭–Bdim7–C–C♯dim7–Dm7
- F–Fsus–F–Fsus2–F–B♭–B♭sus–B♭–B♭sus2–B♭–C–Csus–C–Csus2–C
- G–Em–C–D–Am–Bm–D–G
- Gmaj7–Em7–C7–D7–Am7–Bm7–D7–Gmaj7
- G7–C7–D7–G7
- G9–C9–D9–G9
- G–G+–G6–G7–C–Cm–D–D+7–G

- Gmaj7–G6–Gm7–Gm6–Bm7–Bbm7–Am7–D11–Gm7
- Am7–A11–D13–D13♭9–D13♭5♭9–Gmaj7
- G –G♯dim7–Am–A♯dim7–Bm7–C–C♯dim7–D–D♯dim7–Em
- G–Gsus–G–Gsus2–G–C–Csus–C–Csus2–C–D–Dsus–D–Dsus2–D

This section on chords by degree should be reviewed a few times until you can recite the above chord structures at will. Retake the written lesson if you need to do so. Use blank manuscript paper and check each answer as you go if you feel the need to do so. Do not look up the answer first, then work the exercise. You won't develop your reasoning skills that way.

You have come a long way since that first lesson. Congratulations!

CHORDS BY INTERVALS

HOW INTERVALS WORK

Let's look at the C major scale once again.

Using the degree method, we get the following intervals: From 1 to 2 is a second, from 1 to 3 is a third, 1 to 4 is a fourth, and so on through the scale, with 8 being the octave. Though there are specific names for all intervals, for now we will work on the most basic type of harmony, building chords in thirds. We will focus on two types, the major third (M3) and the minor third (m3).

The major third is found if we play the first note and the move upward to the third note in the major scale.

We see that C-E fills the requirements. C-D is one step, and D-E is one step, so we say that **two whole steps = major third (M3)**. Memorize this now.

If we lower (flat) the E to E♭, we see that the interval has changed to a distance of 1½ steps. This is called a minor third (m3). **So, 1½ steps = m3.** Memorize this now.

N.B. For now, we are talking about notes in ascending order. Notes in descending order have a different approach for naming. We'll discuss that later.

BUILDING CHORDS BY INTERVALS

Here is your first chord formula by interval:

Major triad formula: M3 + m3 or 1-3-5

Look at the chord below. We used the 1-3-5 method to structure a C major chord. Examine the distance between the first and the third; it is a distance of two whole steps, or a major third. Examine the distance between the third and the fifth; it is a distance of 1½ steps, or a minor third. All major chords can be constructed this way.

No matter which way we approach the chord structure of a major chord in any key, the answer will always turn out the same. The degree method is good for recall, the interval method good for playing, improvising, transposing, and finding harmony parts etc.

If you were to go back now and rewrite the answers for all of your major triads using this method, the answers would always be the same.

Minor triad formula: m3 + M3 or 1-♭3-5

Look at the Cm chord below. Notice the distance from C to E♭ is 1½ steps, a m3. The distance from the E♭ to the G is two whole steps, a M3. All minor chords can be constructed this way. Check some previous examples.

Augmented triad formula: M3 + M3 or 1-3-♯5

Look at the C+ triad below. Notice that the distance from C to E is a major third, and the distance from E to G♯ is also a major third. All augmented (+) chords are constructed this way.

Diminished triad formula: m3 + m3 or 1-♭3-♭5

Look at the C° triad below. Notice that C to E♭ is a m3, and the distance from E♭ to G♭ is a m3. All diminished triads can be constructed in this manner.

Memorize all interval and degree formulas at this point. All other chords will be built on one of these four basic triads.

Major seventh chord formula: M3 + m3 +M3 or 1-3-5-7

Dominant seventh chord formula: M3 + m3 +m3 or 1-3-5-♭7

Minor seventh chord formula: m3 + M3 +m3 or 1-♭3-5-♭7

Minor/major seventh chord formula: m3+M3+M3 or 1-♭3-5-7

Major sixth chord formula: M3+m3+M2 or 1-3-5-6

(A whole step is a major second, a half step is a minor second.)

Minor sixth chord formula: m3 + M3 + M2 or 1-♭3-5-6

Half diminished seventh chord formula: m3 +m3+M3 or 1-♭3-♭5-♭7

Fully diminished seventh chord formula: m3 + m3 +m3 or 1-♭3-♭5-♭♭7

Augmented seventh chord formula: M3 + M3 + M2* or 1-3-♯5-♭7

(*This is correctly called a diminished third (d3) and is a whole step, but a major second (M2) might be easier to think of when playing.)

Major ninth chord formula: M3 + m3 +M3 +m3 or 1-3-5-7-9

Dominant ninth chord formula: M3 + m3 +m3 +M3 or 1-3-5-♭7-9

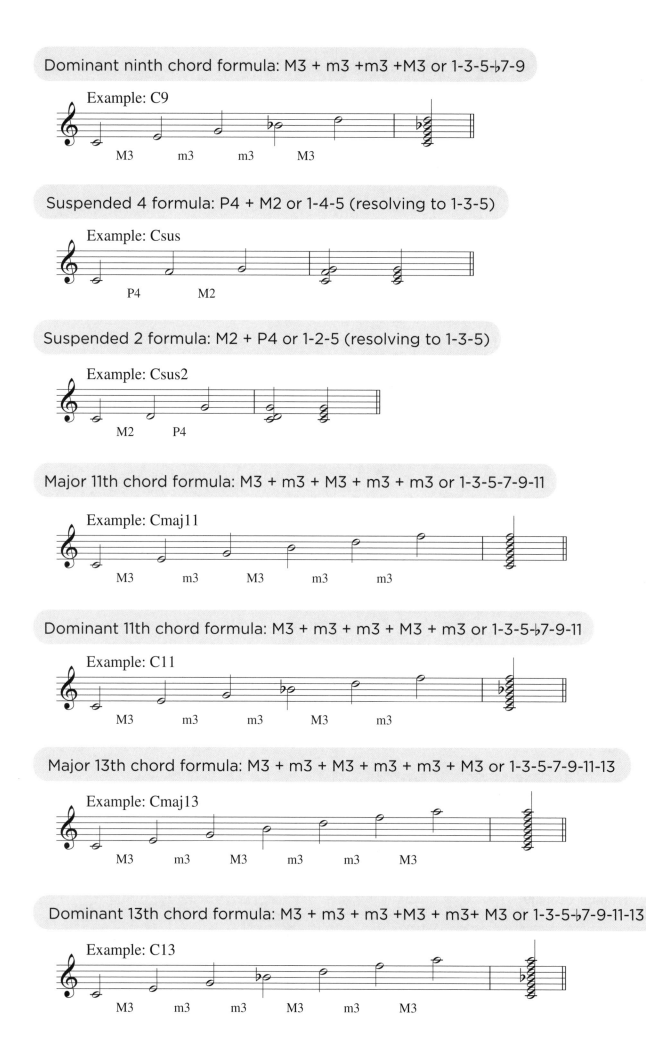

Example: C9

M3   m3   m3   M3

Suspended 4 formula: P4 + M2 or 1-4-5 (resolving to 1-3-5)

Example: Csus

P4   M2

Suspended 2 formula: M2 + P4 or 1-2-5 (resolving to 1-3-5)

Example: Csus2

M2   P4

Major 11th chord formula: M3 + m3 + M3 + m3 + m3 or 1-3-5-7-9-11

Example: Cmaj11

M3   m3   M3   m3   m3

Dominant 11th chord formula: M3 + m3 + m3 + M3 + m3 or 1-3-5-♭7-9-11

Example: C11

M3   m3   m3   M3   m3

Major 13th chord formula: M3 + m3 + M3 + m3 + m3 + M3 or 1-3-5-7-9-11-13

Example: Cmaj13

M3   m3   M3   m3   m3   M3

Dominant 13th chord formula: M3 + m3 + m3 +M3 + m3+ M3 or 1-3-5-♭7-9-11-13

Example: C13

M3   m3   m3   M3   m3   M3

When you get to the 11th and 13th chords, sometimes it is easier to think of them as two separate chords superimposed upon each other.

Example: C13

Try playing an arpeggio of this chord, thinking of it as a C7 chord plus a Dm chord.

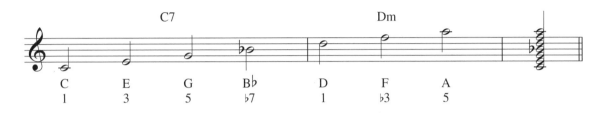

Before moving ahead, take time now to review all chord structures. Commit them to memory and play all in arpeggio form in the key of C.

Can you see that these will form the basis for melody and improvisation of solos?

Now get your blank manuscript paper and do all of these in the following keys:

G   D   A   E   B   F♯   C♯
F   B♭   E♭   A♭   D♭   G♭   C♭

If you get maxed here, do at least the first five sharp keys and the first four flat keys.

BASIC RULES OF INTERVALS

Look at the C major scale below. Each of the degrees has been given a name. It is important know these names, but it is equally important to be able to hear them and know how to use them. That is where the final reward lies.

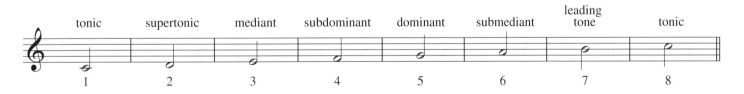

Naming Intervals

- Intervals of second, third, sixth, and seventh are called **major intervals**.
- Intervals of fourth, fifth, unison, and octave are called **perfect intervals**.
- When any of the above intervals are raised a half step, they are **augmented** (+).

- When a major interval is lowered by one half step, it becomes a **minor interval** (not a minor chord). If it is lowered an additional half step, it becomes a **diminished interval** (not a diminished chord).
- When a perfect interval is lowered one half step, it becomes a **diminished interval**.
- A **tritone** interval is three whole steps (e.g., from C up to F♯/G♭).

See examples of these intervals below. Play. Listen. Memorize.

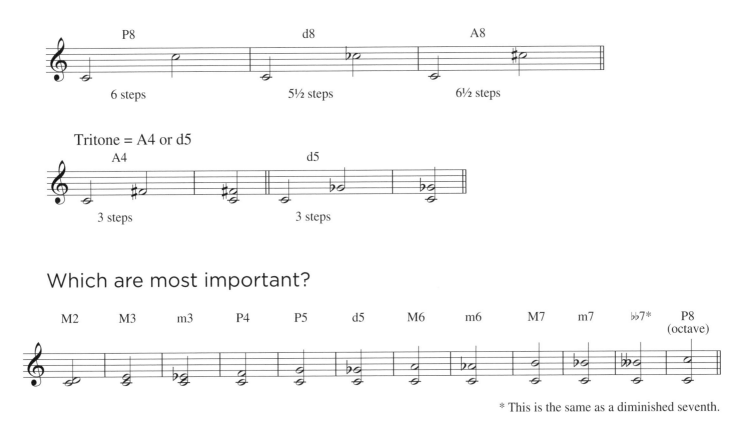

Which are most important?

* This is the same as a diminished seventh.

Compound Intervals

If you take a **simple interval** such as C to D (a major second), and move the D up one octave (8va), you now have a major ninth (M9) interval. Most simple intervals can be made into **compound intervals** by taking them up one octave.

Remember: Second, third, sixth, ninth, 10th, and 13th are all major intervals. The fourth, fifth, 11th, and 12th are perfect intervals. The previous rules for augmentation and diminution (etc.) still apply to these, so it is possible, for instance, to have a minor 10th interval. This is quite common. The John Lennon/Paul McCartney song "Blackbird" contains a number of major and minor 10th intervals.

Ear Training

Play and learn these intervals. You must at this point learn how they sound if you haven't already. This is extremely important, as ear training is essential for all musicians. You then should move on to learning the other intervals by sound. It will take a lot of practice, but you can learn this skill. Get someone to help you, playing interval identification games until you can name them confidently.

Next come the chords. You should be able to identify the chords by sound. Go to the long list of progressions you wrote on blank manuscript paper. Play these again and again until the chord sounds begin to sink into your inner ear.

Inverted Intervals

All intervals can be inverted. The example below shows a M3 (C to E). If we invert this, it becomes E to C. This is no longer a third, but a sixth. Count up from E to C, and you see that it takes six notes, so it is an interval of a sixth of some sort. But we have to work it out with the correct name. Since it is four whole steps, it is a minor sixth (m6).

The second example shows you an interval of a minor third (m3) with the notes E to G. If we invert this interval to show G to E, we discover that it is 4½ steps and thus a major sixth (M6) interval.

This is how inverted intervals are named. Memorize principles. That will save you a lot of grief and annoyance later on.

Memorize the following:

- Major becomes minor.
- Minor becomes major.
- Perfect becomes perfect.
- Augmented becomes diminished.
- Diminished becomes augmented.

All inverted intervals should add up to the number nine:

- A second becomes a seventh: 2 + 7 = 9
- A third becomes a sixth: 3 + 6 = 9
- A fourth becomes a fifth: 4 + 5 = 9
- A fifth becomes a fourth: 5 + 4 = 9
- *et cetera*
- Get it? Okay, great!

Naming Chords

Sometimes, there can be confusion about naming chords. When chords have four, five, six, or more notes chords, it may be possible to label them with more than one chord name. These are the things to consider:

1. What key are you in? (Try not to use flat chords in a sharp key and vice versa.)

2. What is the chord immediately preceding the chord in question?

3. What is the chord following the chord in question?

4. How is the chord used? (Is it a passing or leading chord? An accidental chord? A stand-alone rhythm chord?

Remember: A song with a lot of accidental chords – ♭VII, ♭III, VI, or a lot of diminished chords – can take on a polytonal character. ("Polytonal" means the composer is using more than two different keys at the same time.) Name the chords with the four questions above in mind. Use the number system – to be explained in Section C – which gives you a progression that is easily transposed to new keys. Experience will help you work this out as time goes on.

CHORDS IN KEYS

Chords in and of themselves, without knowing how and when to use them, can be practically useless. You must know how to employ them within the context of the key, song, and progression, and what effect they will have. Let's apply what we have learned to chords in within keys.

TRIADS

There are predictable chords (triads) given to each key by the harmonized scales of the key. You must know these as they occur in the key. All progressions have their basis here.

Then we will make seventh chords (four notes), and look at substitutions and altered chords, used for melody chords and for creating bass lines.

No matter what style of music, you must memorize the triads in the keys that are most likely to be used.

The Number System

Look at the harmonized major scales below. The first uses only thirds, while the second uses full triads.

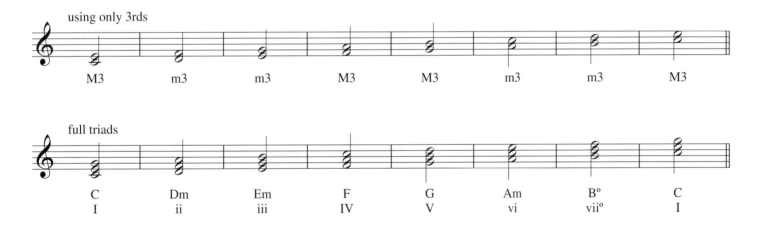

When we examine the first chord directly above, we see M3 + m3. This is a major chord, C major. We will now designate it as the I (one) chord.

Major chords are represented by upper-case Roman numerals.

When we examine the second chord, we see it is m3 + M3. This is a minor chord, Dm, now represented as ii.

Minor chords are represented by lower-case Roman numerals.

When we examine the third chord, we see m3 + M3: E minor, iii.

When we examine the fourth chord, we see M3 + m3: F major, IV

When we examine the fifth chord we see M3 + m3: G major, V.

When we examine the sixth chord we see m3 + M3: A minor, vi.

When we examine the seventh chord, we see m3 + m3: B diminished, vii°.

The eighth chord is the same as the first: C major, I.

So, we have the following:

- I, IV, and V are major chords in the key.
- ii, iii, and vi are minor chords in the key.
- vii° is the diminished chord in the key.

This sequence occurs in every major key, every time!

Note: Studio musicians and good live musicians use the number system all the time. It is great for transposing song progressions to a new key instantly.

Triads in the Major Scales

In any song, the progression will always be the same numerically, in all keys at the same time. What does that mean? Consider this example of a standard progression:

I–vi–IV–V in C = C–Am–F–G

I–vi–IV–V in G = G–Em–C–D

Harmonize the G major scale into triads below.

You should have: G = I; Am = ii; Bm = iii; C = IV; D= V; Em = vi; F#° = vii°; G = I

So a I–vi–IV–V progression in G is G–Em–C–D. It checks out!

Write the following keys in triads.

D major

A major

E major

B major

F♯ major

C♯ major

F major

B♭ major

E♭ major

A♭ major

Db major

Gb major

Cb major

Triads in the Minor Scales

Now you know the major scale triads. What about the minor scale triads?

A natural minor

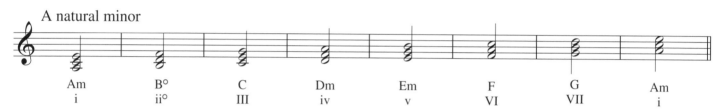

| Am | B° | C | Dm | Em | F | G | Am |
| i | ii° | III | iv | v | VI | VII | i |

As you see above, A natural minor has the same triads as C major.

For the harmonic minor, there are three new chords, all with the #7 (G#) affected. We will call them C+ (III+), E (V), and G#° (#vii°).

A harmonic minor

| Am | B° | C+ | Dm | E | F | G#° | Am |
| i | ii° | III+ | iv | V | VI | #vii° | i |

For the melodic minor, we add three more new chords, all with the F# affected. They are Bm (ii), D (IV), and F#° (#vi°).

A melodic minor

| Am | Bm | C+ | D | E | F#° | G#° | Am |
| i | ii | III+ | IV | V | #vi° | #vii° | i |

THE BASIC CHORDS IN EVERY KEY

You need to know how to play all the chords in a particular key by recall and by sound. A song will not use all of these, only a few, depending upon the style. Does this mean that these are the only chords we can use for a song in a particular key? No, not at all! Remember, the composer can use and alter whatever chords she chooses to get the effect needed.

That last sentence is very important. Chords should get effect! Choose the right one and the job is accomplished. That's easier said than done, however, so read on.

Here are some common chord substitutions used in songs. They may require sharps and flats that are not in the key signature, however.

	In C major
I or i	C or Cm
IV or iv	F or Fm
V or V+7	G or G+7
iii or ♭III	Em or E♭
vii° or ♭VII	B° or B♭
vi or VI or vi(maj7)	Am or A or Am(maj7)
vi or ♭VI	Am or A♭
♯V to V	G♯ to G

You have heard some or all of these in songs you know and love. Try substituting chords to see what you hear, like:

	In C major
♭VI–♭VII–I	A♭–B♭–C
I–vi–iv–V–I	C–Am–Fm–G–C
I–vi–IV–iv–V– I	C–Am–F–Fm–G–C

SEVENTH CHORDS

Now let's expand the triads to seventh chords (four notes) and see what kind of seventh chords we get in the key.

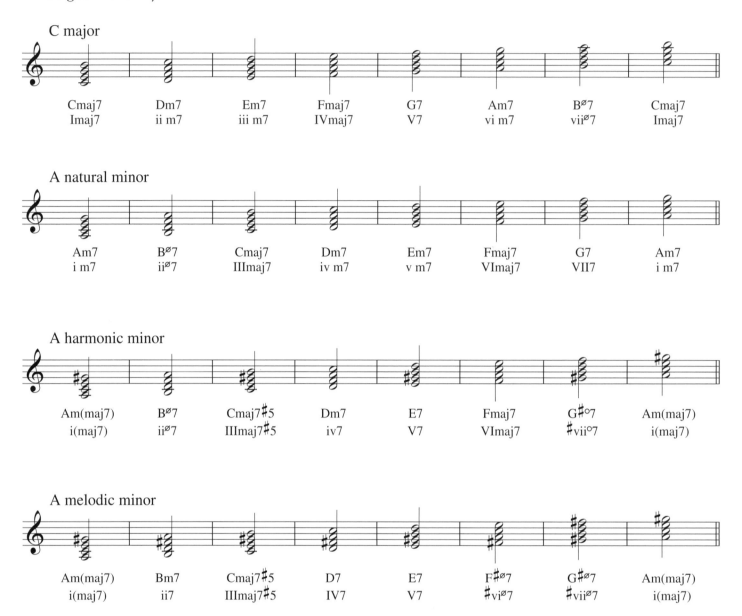

Sevenths add texture and conflict or smoothness, depending upon the style of music. Rock 'n' roll likes the dominant seventh chords, jazz likes the major seventh chords. Diminished seventh chords are leading tone chords to take you to another chord.

Review everything up to this point. Play the triads in every key, then play the seventh chords in every key.

Write the seventh chords in the key below.

G major

D major

A major

E major

B major

F♯ major

C♯ major

F major

B♭ major

E♭ major

The next logical step is to write the seventh chords for all the minor scales. This can become tedious, so write them at your leisure in your manuscript book. Check the chord structures to see if they match up with the examples.

SECTION D

CHORD PROGRESSIONS & SUBSTITUTIONS

We have been working our way toward chord progressions and how to choose a good substitute chord if:

- The chord progression becomes stale.
- You need to find a chord with the melody as the high note.
- You need to find a chord with the bass line as a low note.
- You need a chord that provides you with the high melody note and the low bass note at the same time (the best type of chord substitution).

In the process, you should train your ear to recognize all types of progressions and chords, but this process can be helpful for guitarists or others wishing to play a lead sheet (fake book) arrangement that has only the melody and chords. You can experiment with a melody, chords, and a bass line to find a unique arrangement on almost any tune. This may mean transposing to another key to find the needed chord substitutions so that the arrangement comes out the way you want it to sound. This is one of my favorite things to do.

Before you can do the substitutions effectively, you need to know

- the scale
- the key signature
- the basic chords in the key
- how to structure, by degree or interval, all the chords you may need
- the following guidelines for substituting chords

Let's list them here. We will refer to each and use specific examples that will show you how to work them yourself. This information is important, so if you get confused take some time to make sure you have a firm grasp of the items cited above.

RULES FOR CHORD SUBSTITUTION

1. The easiest way to find a substitution is to use basically the same chord, but with a new "voice." For example:

- G   or Gmaj7
- G   or G7
- G   or G6
- Gm   or Gm6
- Gm   or Gm7

This depends upon the style of music, so use your ear.

2. A substitute chord must have at least two notes in common. This is another easy to way to find several possible substitutions. Keep the key in context, and the style of music. Don't use the first thing you run across. Try a few before deciding.

3. A substitute chord must act in the same manner. Occasionally there will be a non-diatonic passing chord between two diatonic chords in a progression. This could be a diminished chord, for example, that adds texture between two chords momentarily. A substitute chord may have one or two notes in common – non-diatonic and acting in the same manner – and these are okay. Use discretion.

Take note, however, that these chords may not be played together with the regular chord in the progression, as the previous examples may, but only in place of it. If someone else is playing the traditional expected chord and you substitute the new chord, you may hear a clash – and get some dirty looks. Talk it over with the other instrumentalists and let them know you are substituting the chord. If you are the only one playing chords, go for it!

4. When substituting against a major/minor seventh chord, especially the V7 chord, use its v7 as a substitute. Here's an example in C major:

G7 is the V7 in the key.

- Use Dm7 as the substitute. The bass should remain on G, however. This gives the chord the sound of a dominant 11th chord.
- G7 = G-B-D-F (1-3-5-♭7)
- Dm7 = D-F-A-C
- G11 = G-B-D-F-A-C (1-3-5-♭7-9-11)

A v6 would also give you a dominant ninth chord.

- G7 = G-B-D-F (1-3-5-♭7)
- Dm6 = D-F-A-B
- G9 = G-B-D-F-A (1-3-5-♭7-9)

This is a tough one to recognize at first. Just remember, if it's a major/minor seventh chord, especially the V7, use the v7 as a substitution.

5. Use extended chords as substitutions. If the chord is a C7, try:

C9   C11   C13   C13♭5   C13♭5(♭9)   C7♯5(♭9)   *etc.*

Find the chord and inversion that will allow you to fit the high note of the melody or the low note of the bass line – or both – into the chord you are looking for. This is the essence of the whole idea. If you know this material, you can play chords, melody, and bass and get a total arrangement of the piece.

Not all songs lend themselves to all of the above rules. Country, rock 'n' roll, and classical music will require conservative changes to their chord progressions. Jazz and contemporary arrangements lend themselves to more creative substitutions of chords.

Also remember, the melody may not always be in the underlying rhythm chord structure. Melody always takes precedence if you are playing chord-melody arrangements. It must be there. Adapt the chord as needed to fit the melody into the chord as the highest note – it's easier to hear that way – or the lowest note in the chord, which will also work.

The bass line can be interwoven into the chord progression also. This brings in the altered and extended chords, as the bass line may often be the ♭5 or ♭9 in the chord. This is quite common in jazz-type arrangements.

> Tip: Get the high melody note and then the low bass note and fit the chord to the progression by filling in the blanks.

EXAMPLES OF CHORD SUBSTITUTION

Look at the underlying chord as needed and apply one of the five rules of substitution. This will allow you to find some very interesting chords. If a particular chord is not in your chord book, don't worry. Use it anyway, as long as it sounds good in context with the progression and is used in a musical way. Some of the chords you discover may sound dissonant when played by themselves, but that is not how you are using them. They will be in context with the progression.

Let's look at the example below.

standard progression

substitution

Assign these to number sequences and transpose to the following keys:

G   D   A   E   F   B♭   E♭   A♭

Which rules of substitution did we use?

measure 1: Rule 1
2: Rule 1
3: Rule 1
4: Rule 3
5: Rule 1
6: Rule 4 first chord
Rule 5 second chord

7: Rule 1 first chord
Rule 3 second chord
8: Rule 1 first chord
Rule 5 second chord

Let's look at another progression:

standard progression

substitution

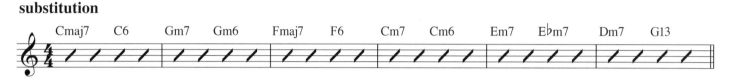

Assign these to number sequences and transpose to the following keys:

G D A E F B♭ E♭ A B

Which rules of substitution did we use?

measure 1: Rule 1
2: Rule 4
3: Rule 1
4: Rule 1
5: Rule 2 first chord
Rule 3 second chord
6: Rule 1 first chord
Rule 5 second chord

Still More Substitutions

old

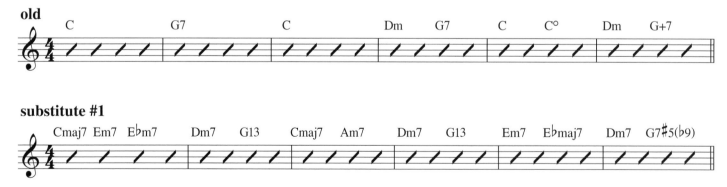

substitute #1

substitute #2

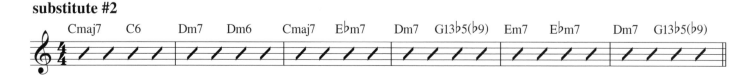

old

substitute #1

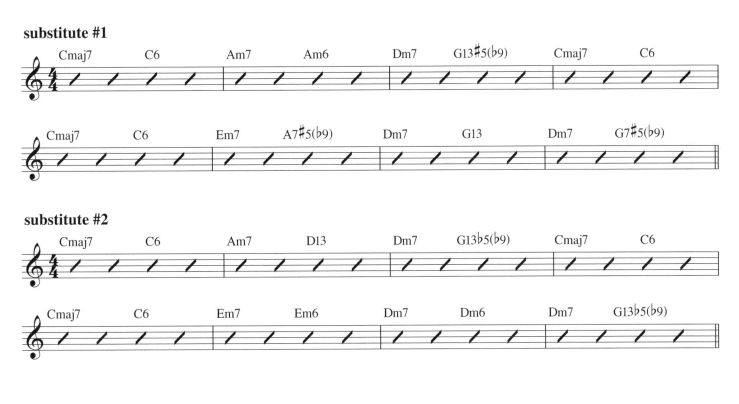

substitute #2

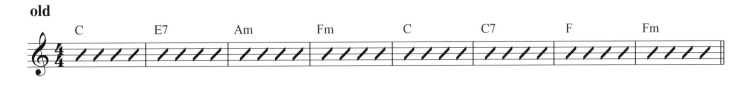

old

substitute #1

substitute #2

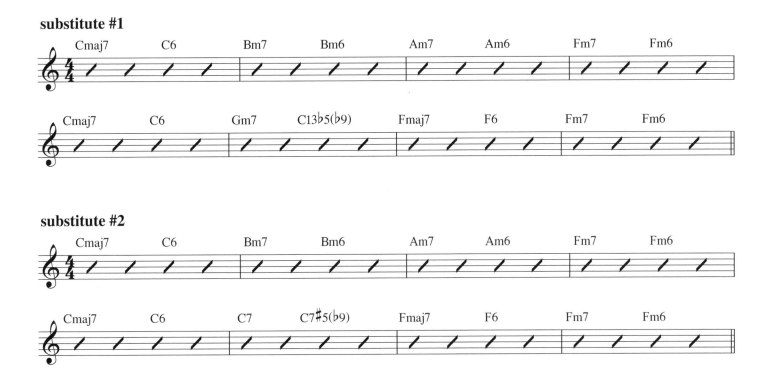

Assignment

Get some blank manuscript paper and go back and give all these last progressions the number treatment. Transpose them to the following keys, at least.

G   D   A   E   B   F   B♭   E♭

You need write the number sequence only one time to transpose it to all keys. Try to do the transposition in your head. Work one key at a time. This will not be an easy task, but stick with it until you can do it. It will take some time, but you *can* do it.

CONCLUSION

Congratulations! This has not been an easy task. If you have stuck with the plan all along, you will have a good companion to take with you the rest of the way on your journey through the difficult maze of music theory.

If you became sidetracked, that's still okay. You can always go back and rework whatever you feel you need to. With the answers in the back, it's easy to see where you went wrong. Good luck in all your musical endeavors.

ANSWER SECTION

ANSWER SECTION

This section contains answers to the quizzes, some written scales and chords, etc. Use this only to check your work. Don't look up the answers first! Use a pencil so you can erase incorrect answers and write them again. Additionally, you might wish to purchase a blank manuscript book and write the answers as frequently as needed.

CHART OF KEY SIGNATURES (treble clef only)

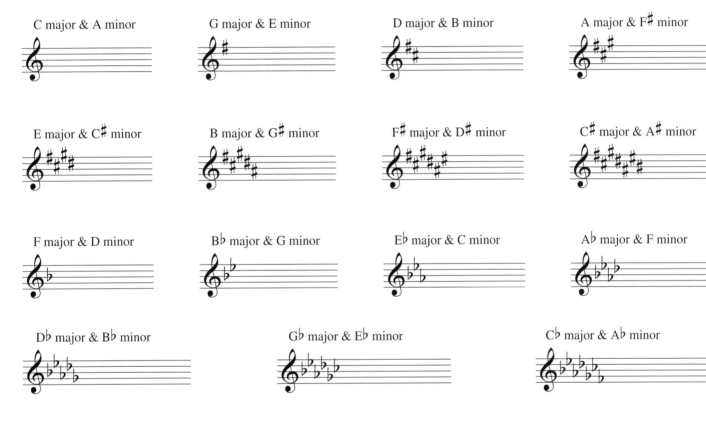

SECTION A: The Sharp Keys

DIRECTORY OF ALL THE SHARP MAJOR SCALES

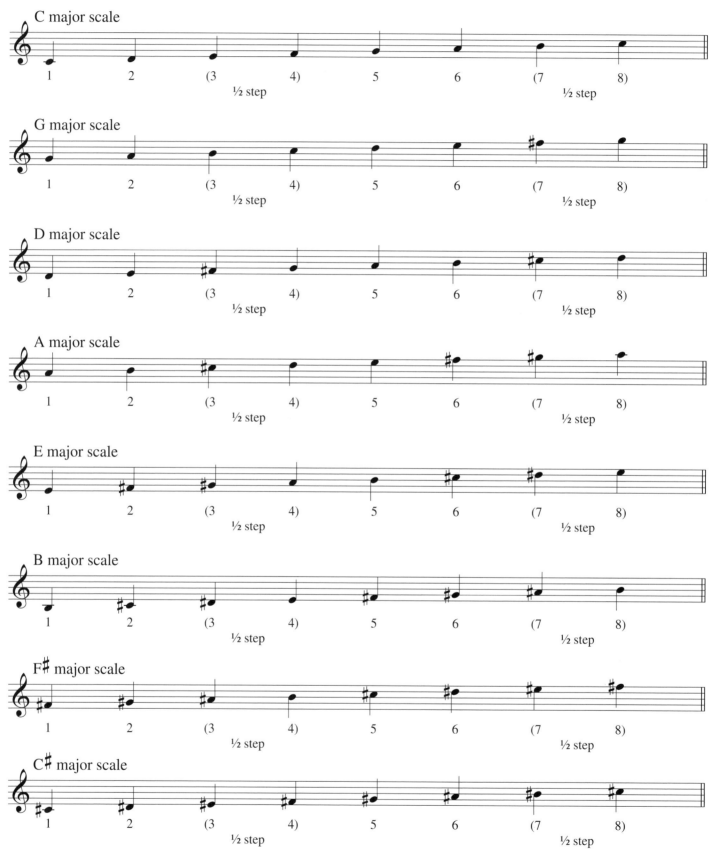

QUIZ 1
1. C
2. E
3. G
4. B
5. F
6. D
7. A
8. no sharps, no flats

QUIZ 2
1. G
2. B
3. D
4. F♯
5. C
6. A
7. E
8. one sharp: F♯, 7th degree

QUIZ 3
1. D
2. F♯
3. A
4. C♯
5. G
6. E
7. B
8. two sharps: F♯, 3rd degree;
   C♯, 7th degree

QUIZ 4
1. A
2. C♯
3. E
4. G♯
5. D
6. B
7. F♯
8. C♯, F♯, G♯; 3rd, 6th, 7th

QUIZ 5
1. E
2. G♯
3. B
4. D♯
5. A
6. F♯
7. C♯
8. F♯, G♯, C♯, D♯;
   2nd, 3rd, 6th, 7th

9. C♯, F♯, G♯
10. F♯, C♯
11. F♯
12. no sharps, no flats

QUIZ 6
1. B
2. D♯
3. F♯
4. A♯
5. E
6. C♯
7. G♯
8. C♯, D♯, F♯, G♯, A♯
   2nd, 3rd, 5th, 6th, 7th

QUIZ 7
1. F♯
2. A♯
3. C♯
4. E♯
5. B
6. G♯
7. D♯
8. F♯, G♯, A♯, C♯, D♯, E♯
   1st, 2nd, 3rd, 5th, 6th, 7th

QUIZ 8
1. C♯
2. E♯
3. G♯
4. B♯
5. F♯
6. D♯
7. A♯
8. C♯, D♯, E♯, F♯, G♯, A♯, B♯

   1st, 2nd, 3rd, 4th, 5th, 6th, 7th

9. F♯, G♯, A♯, C♯, D♯, E♯
10. C♯, D♯, F♯, G♯, A♯
11. F♯, G♯, C♯, D♯
12. C♯, F♯, G♯
13. F♯, C♯
14. F♯
15. no sharps, no flats

SECTION B: The Flat Keys

DIRECTORY OF ALL THE FLAT MAJOR SCALES

QUIZ 9
1. F
2. A
3. C
4. E
5. B♭
6. G
7. D
8. B♭

QUIZ 10
1. B♭
2. D
3. F
4. A
5. E♭
6. C
7. G
8. B♭, E♭; 1st, 4th

QUIZ 11
1. E♭
2. G
3. B♭
4. D
5. A♭
6. F
7. C
8. E♭, A♭, B♭; 1st, 4th, 5th

QUIZ 12
1. A♭
2. C
3. E♭
4. G
5. D♭
6. B♭
7. F
8. A♭, B♭, D♭, E♭;
   1st, 2nd, 4th, 5th

QUIZ 13
1. D♭
2. F
3. A♭
4. C
5. G♭
6. E♭
7. B♭
8. D♭, E♭, G♭, A♭, B♭;
   1st, 2nd, 4th, 5th, 6th

QUIZ 14
1. G♭
2. B♭
3. D♭
4. F
5. C♭
6. A♭
7. E♭
8. G♭, A♭, B♭, C♭, D♭, E♭;
   1st, 2nd, 3rd, 4th, 5th, 6th

QUIZ 15
1. C♭
2. E♭
3. G♭
4. B♭
5. F♭
6. D♭
7. A♭
8. C♭, D♭, E♭, F♭, G♭, A♭, B♭
   1st, 2nd, 3rd, 4th, 5th, 6th, 7th

SECTION C: Minor Keys

Page 26

A natural minor

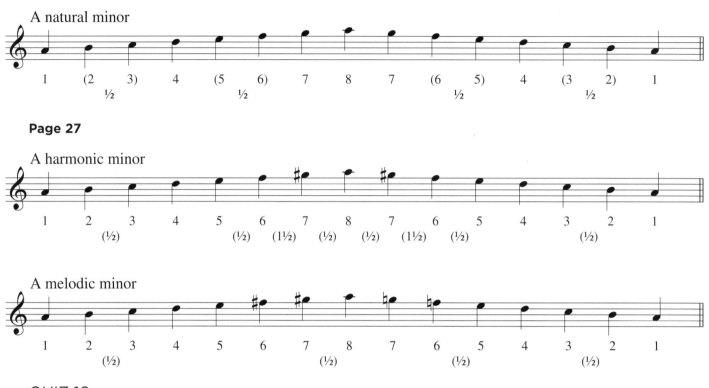

Page 27

A harmonic minor

A melodic minor

QUIZ 16

1. C major

2. half steps at (2-3) and (5-6)

3. half steps at (2-3), (5-6), and (7-8); 1-1/2 steps at (6-7)

4. half steps at (2-3) & (7-8) ascending; half steps at (6-5) and (3-2) descending

5. The tonal center is the apparent "home" or "resting place" of a scale or melody, giving a sense of the "key." The tonal center is the first degree of the scale.

Page 29

E natural minor scale

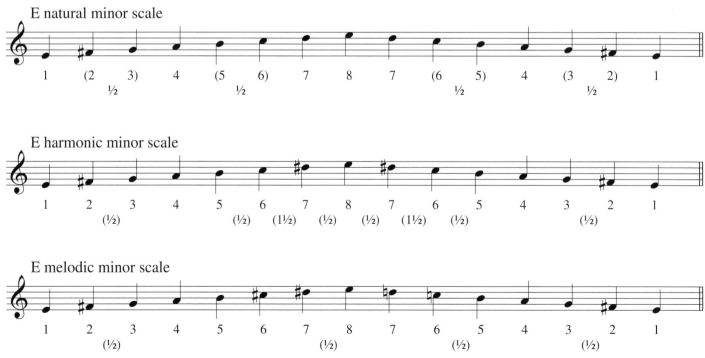

E harmonic minor scale

E melodic minor scale

QUIZ 17

1. E minor
2. F♯
3. D♯
4. C♯
5. D♯

Page 30

B natural minor scale

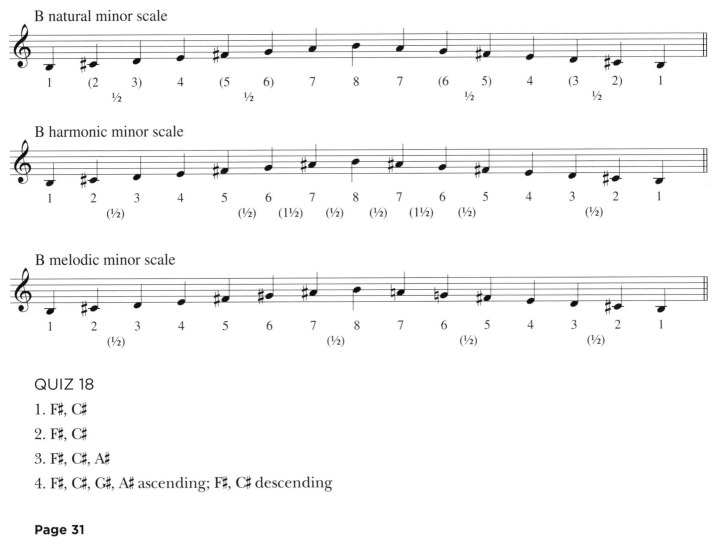

B harmonic minor scale

B melodic minor scale

QUIZ 18

1. F♯, C♯
2. F♯, C♯
3. F♯, C♯, A♯
4. F♯, C♯, G♯, A♯ ascending; F♯, C♯ descending

Page 31

F♯ natural minor scale

F♯ harmonic minor scale

F♯ melodic minor scale

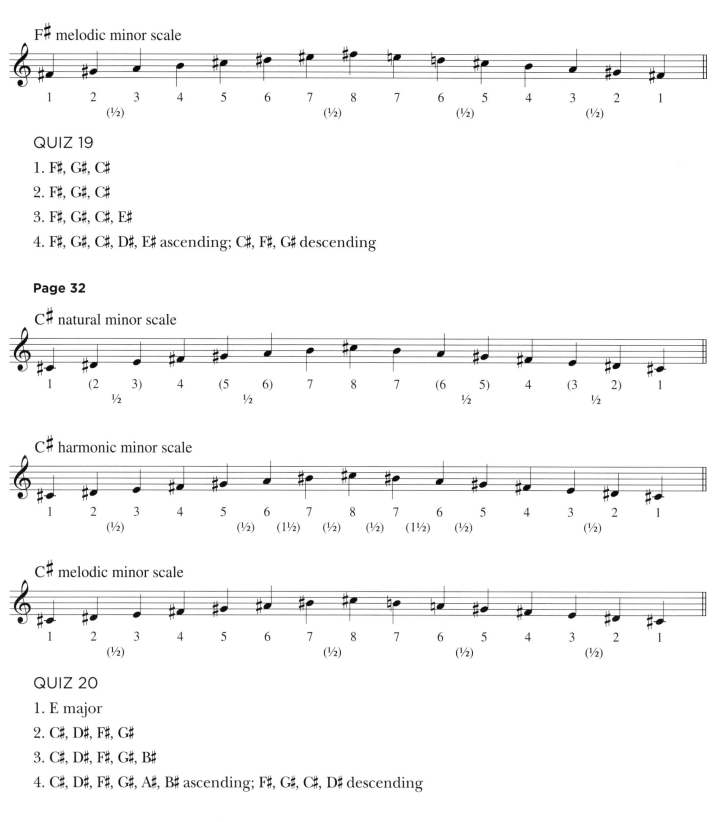

QUIZ 19

1. F♯, G♯, C♯

2. F♯, G♯, C♯

3. F♯, G♯, C♯, E♯

4. F♯, G♯, C♯, D♯, E♯ ascending; C♯, F♯, G♯ descending

Page 32

C♯ natural minor scale

C♯ harmonic minor scale

C♯ melodic minor scale

QUIZ 20

1. E major

2. C♯, D♯, F♯, G♯

3. C♯, D♯, F♯, G♯, B♯

4. C♯, D♯, F♯, G♯, A♯, B♯ ascending; F♯, G♯, C♯, D♯ descending

Page 33

G♯ natural minor scale

G♯ harmonic minor scale

QUIZ 21

1. B major

2. G♯. A♯, C♯, D♯, F♯

3. G♯, A♯, C♯, D♯, F𝄪

4. G♯, A♯, C♯, D♯, E♯, F𝄪 ascending; G♯, A♯, C♯, D♯, F♯ descending

Page 34

D♯ natural minor scale

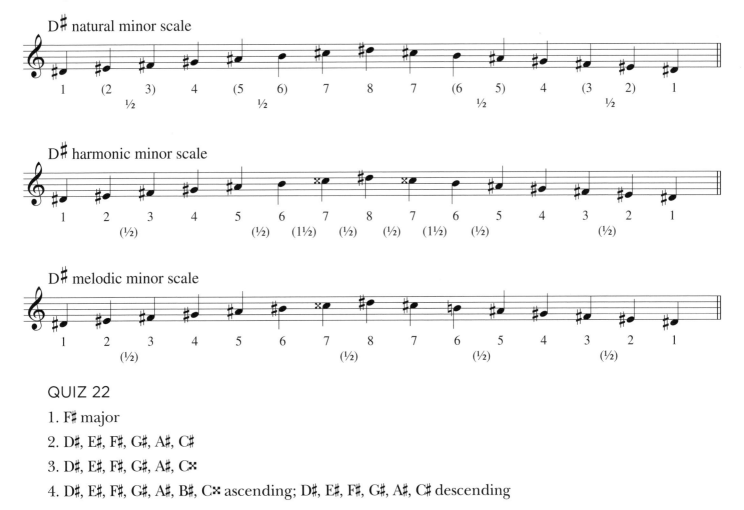

QUIZ 22

1. F♯ major

2. D♯, E♯, F♯, G♯, A♯, C♯

3. D♯, E♯, F♯, G♯, A♯, C𝄪

4. D♯, E♯, F♯, G♯, A♯, B♯, C𝄪 ascending; D♯, E♯, F♯, G♯, A♯, C♯ descending

Page 35

A♯ natural minor scale

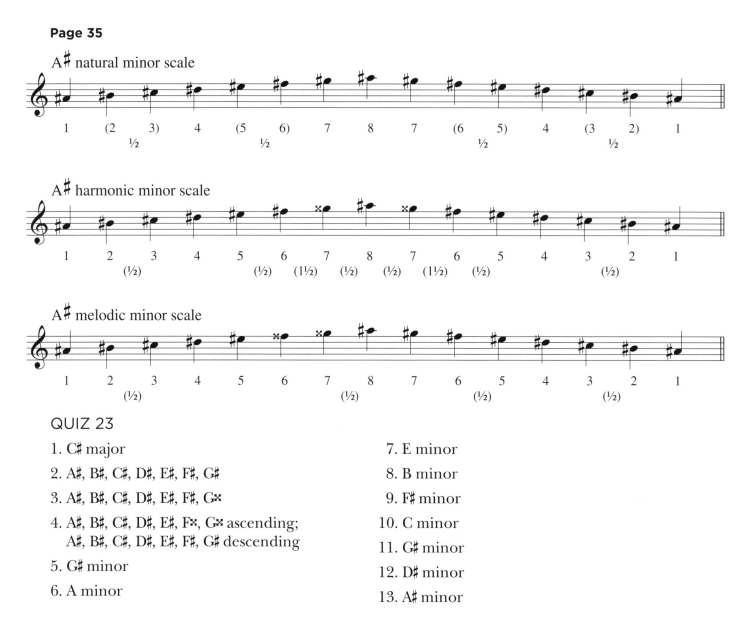

QUIZ 23

1. C♯ major

2. A♯, B♯, C♯, D♯, E♯, F♯, G♯

3. A♯, B♯, C♯, D♯, E♯, F♯, G𝄪

4. A♯, B♯, C♯, D♯, E♯, F𝄪, G𝄪 ascending;
   A♯, B♯, C♯, D♯, E♯, F♯, G♯ descending

5. G♯ minor

6. A minor

7. E minor

8. B minor

9. F♯ minor

10. C minor

11. G♯ minor

12. D♯ minor

13. A♯ minor

Page 37

D natural minor scale

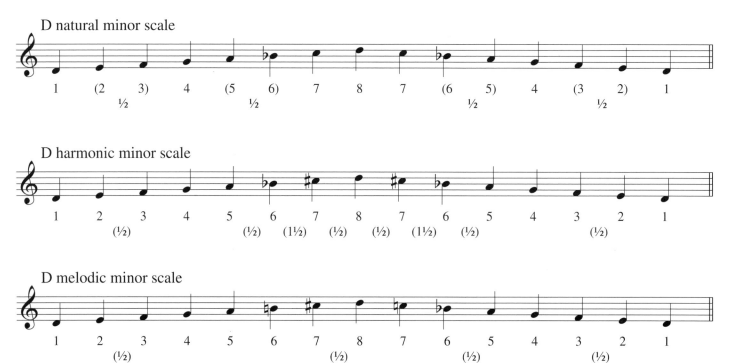

QUIZ 24

1. F major

2. B♭

3. none

4. C♯

5. C♯, and also B♮ ascending; only B♭ descending

Page 38

G natural minor scale

1   (2)   3)   4   (5)   6)   7   8   7   (6)   5)   4   (3)   2)   1
      ½   ½   ½   ½

G harmonic minor scale

1   2   3   4   5   6   7   8   7   6   5   4   3   2   1
    (½)   (½) (1½) (½)   (½) (1½) (½)   (½)

G melodic minor scale

1   2   3   4   5   6   7   8   7   6   5   4   3   2   1
    (½)   (½)   (½)   (½)

QUIZ 25

1. B♭ major

2. none

3. F♯

4. F♯

5. E♮ ascending; E♭ descending

Page 39

C natural minor scale

1   (2)   3)   4   (5)   6)   7   8   7   (6)   5)   4   (3)   2)   1
      ½   ½   ½   ½

C harmonic minor scale

1   2   3   4   5   6   7   8   7   6   5   4   3   2   1
    (½)   (½) (1½) (½)   (½) (1½) (½)   (½)

C melodic minor scale

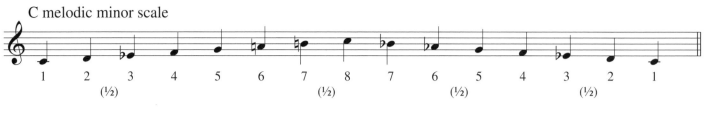

QUIZ 26

1. E♭ major

2. none

3. B♮

4. A♮ and B♮ ascending; A♭ and B♭ descending

Page 40

F natural minor scale

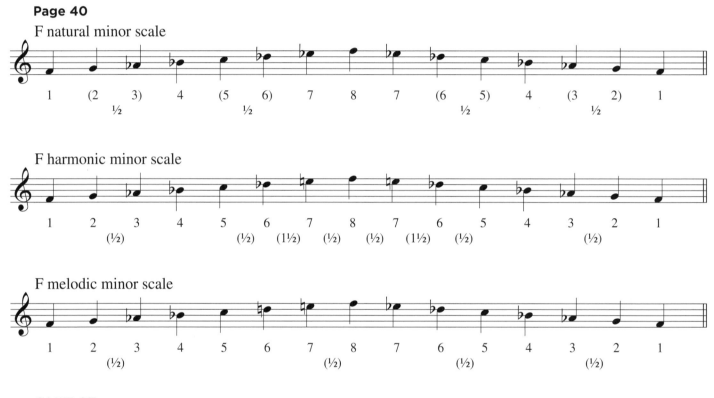

F harmonic minor scale

F melodic minor scale

QUIZ 27

1. A♭ is the relative major key; key signature: A♭, B♭, D♭, E♭

2. none

3. E♭ is changed to E♮.

4. D♭ is changed to D♮, also E♮ ascending; E♭ and D♭ descending

Page 41

B♭ natural minor scale

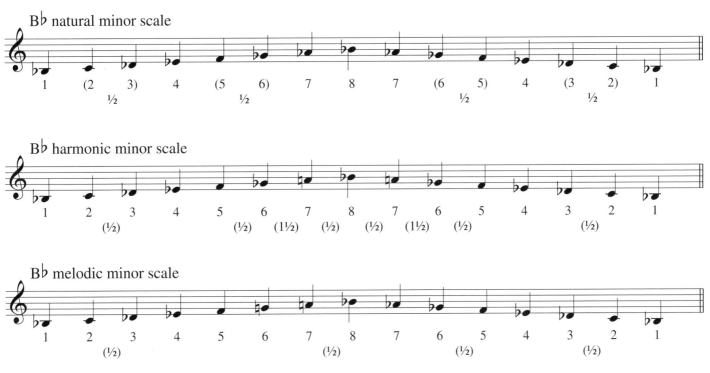

B♭ harmonic minor scale

B♭ melodic minor scale

QUIZ 28

1. D♭ is the relative major key; key signature: D♭, E♭, G♭, A♭, B♭

2. none

3. A♭ becomes A♮

4. G♭ becomes G♮, also A♮ ascending; G♭ and A♭ descending

Page 42

E♭ natural minor scale

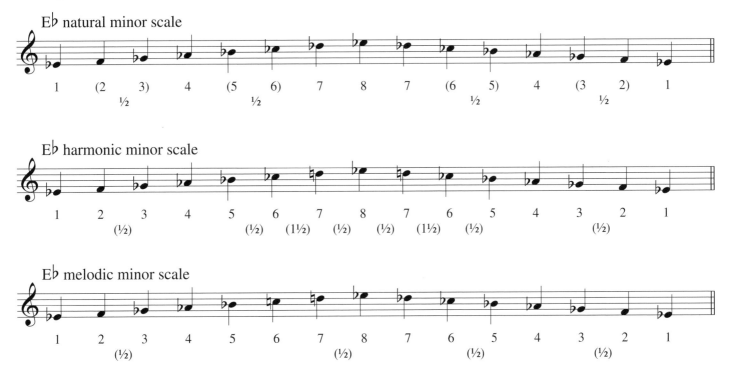

E♭ harmonic minor scale

E♭ melodic minor scale

QUIZ 29

1. G♭ is the relative major key; key signature: G♭, A♭, B♭, C♭, D♭, E♭

2. none

3. D♭ becomes D♮

4. C♭ becomes C♮, also D♮ ascending; D♭ and C♭ descending

Page 43

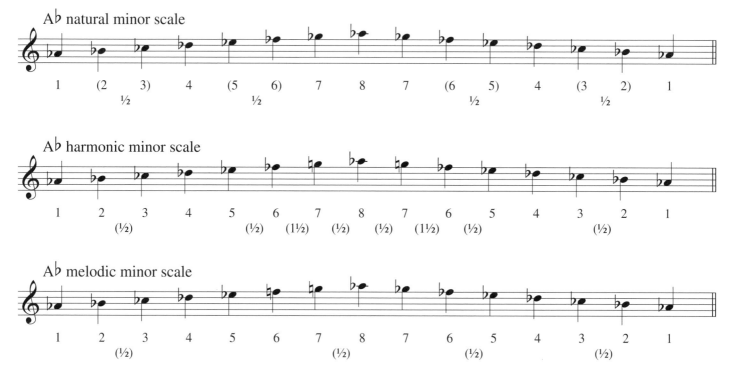

QUIZ 30

1. C♭ is the relative major key; key signature: C♭, D♭, E♭, F♭, G♭, A♭, B♭

2. none

3. G♭ becomes G♮

4. F♭ becomes F♮, also G♮ ascending; G♭ and F♭ descending

Page 44
PENTATONIC SCALES

G major pentatonic

D major pentatonic

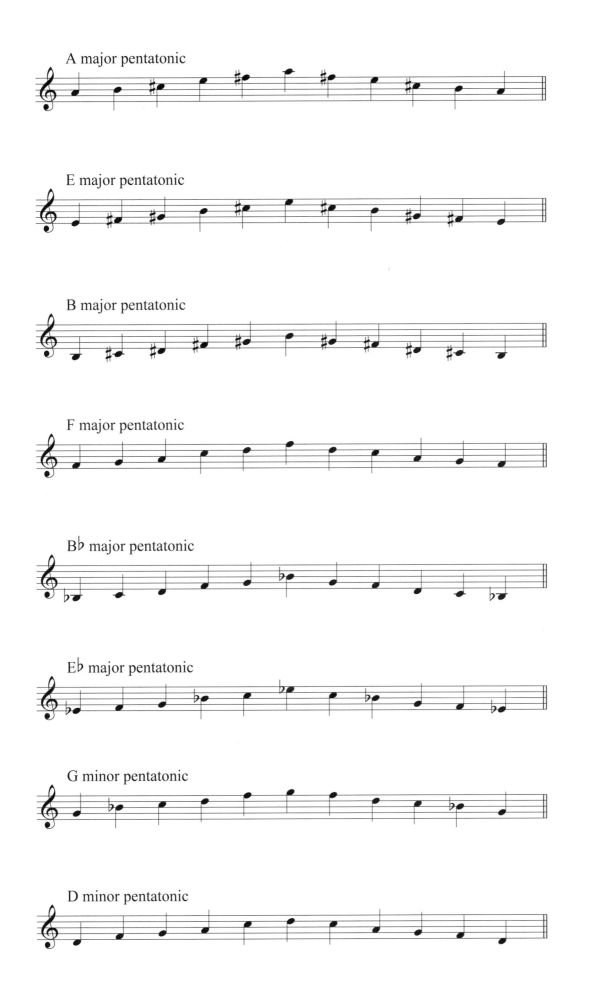

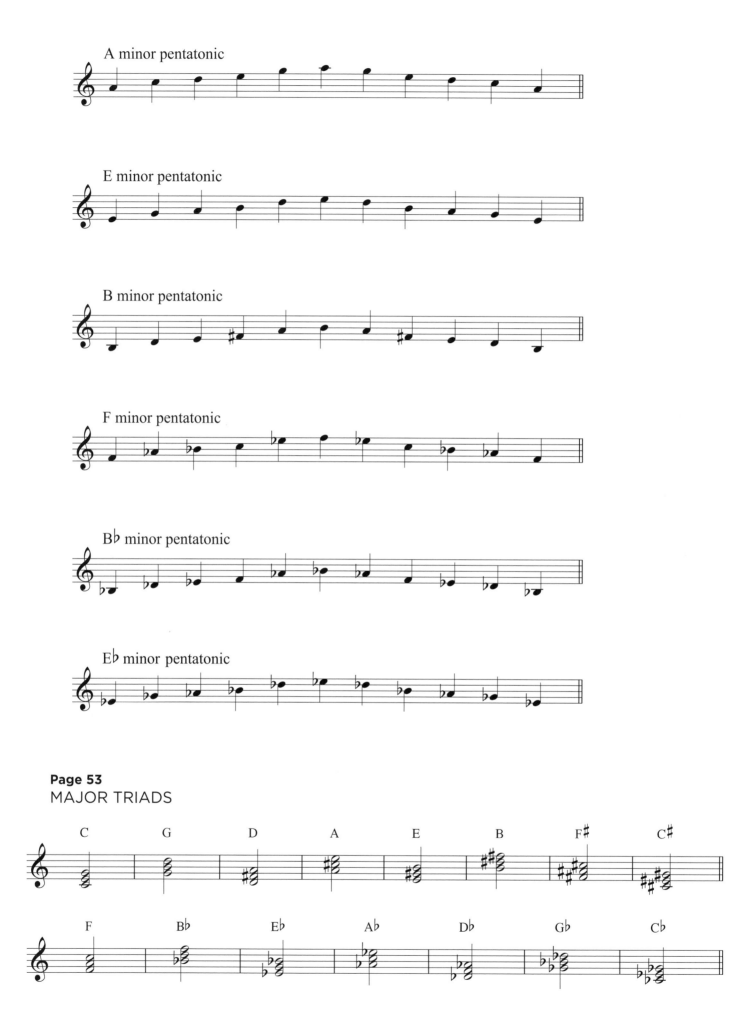

Page 53
MAJOR TRIADS

Page 54
MINOR TRIADS

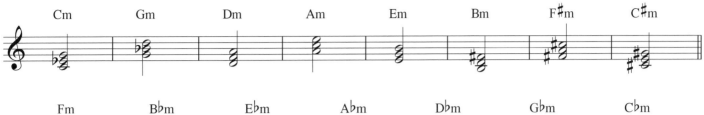

DIMINISHED TRIADS

Page 55
AUGMENTED TRIADS

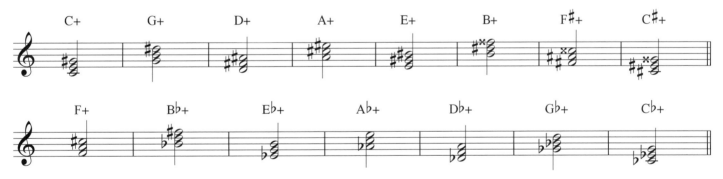

Page 56
MAJOR SEVENTH CHORDS

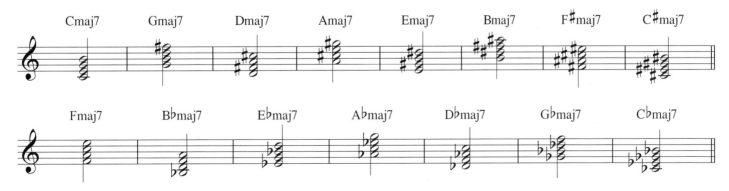

Page 57
DOMINANT SEVENTH CHORDS

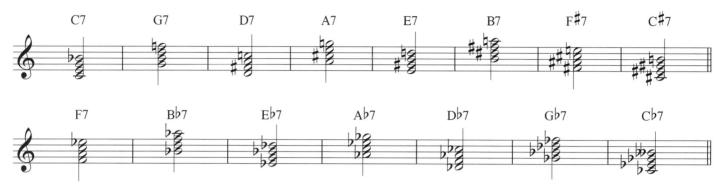

MINOR SEVENTH CHORDS

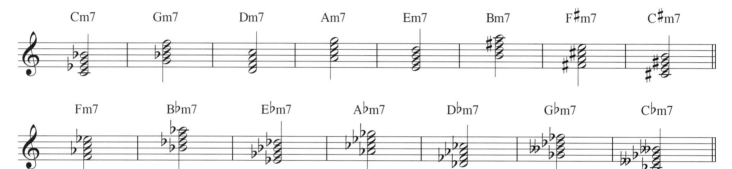

Page 58
MINOR/MAJOR SEVENTH CHORDS

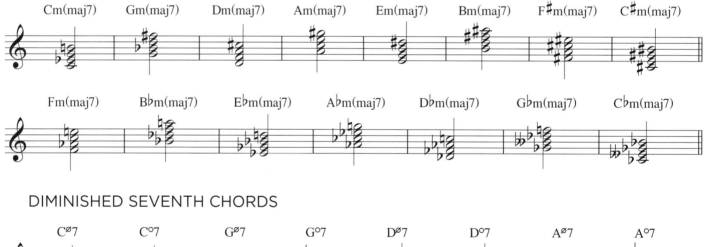

DIMINISHED SEVENTH CHORDS

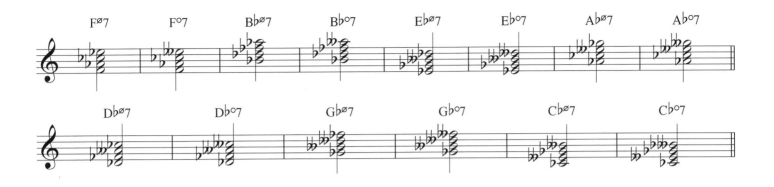

Page 59
AUGMENTED SEVENTH CHORDS

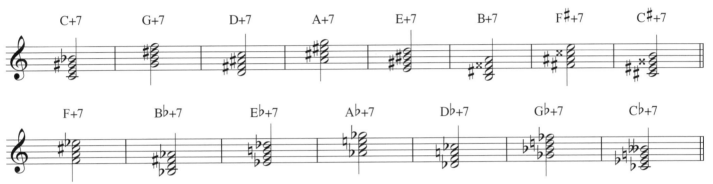

Page 60
MAJOR SIXTH CHORDS

MINOR SIXTH CHORDS

Page 61
MAJOR NINTH CHORDS

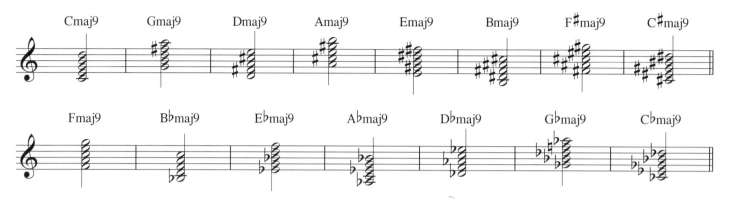

Page 62
DOMINANT NINTH CHORDS

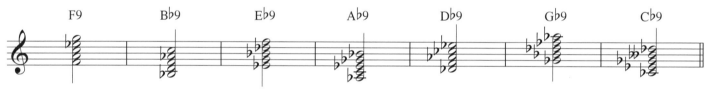

MINOR NINTH CHORDS

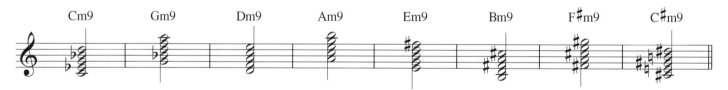

Page 63
MAJOR 11TH & DOMINANT 11TH CHORDS

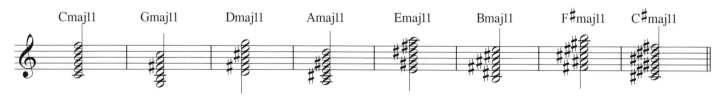

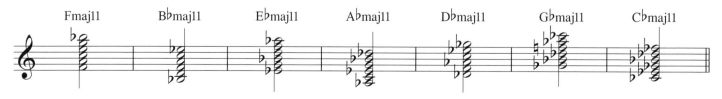

Page 64
MAJOR 13TH & DOMINANT 13TH CHORDS

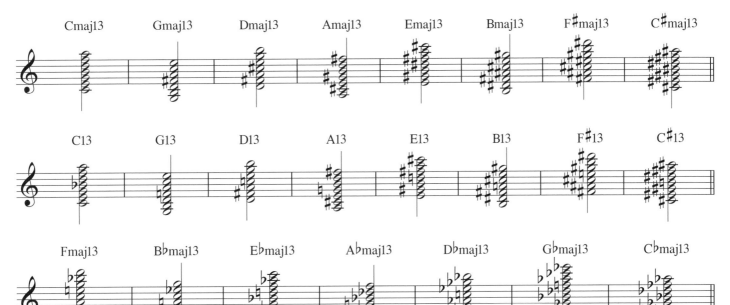

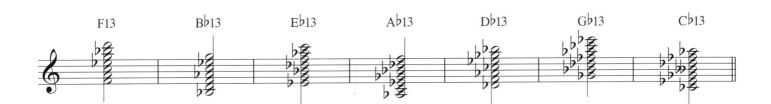

Page 80
MAJOR SCALES HARMONIZIED WITH TRIADS

harmonized G scale with triads

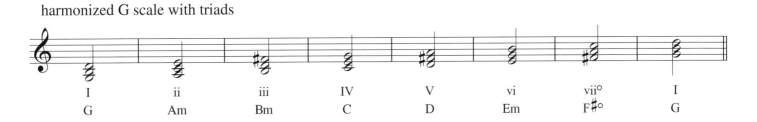

	I	ii	iii	IV	V	vi	vii°	I
	G	Am	Bm	C	D	Em	F#°	G

Page 81

harmonized D scale with triads

I	ii	iii	IV	V	vi	vii°	I
D	Em	F#m	G	A	Bm	C#°	D

harmonized A scale with triads

I	ii	iii	IV	V	vi	vii°	I
A	Bm	C#m	D	E	F#m	G#°	A

harmonized E scale with triads

I	ii	iii	IV	V	vi	vii°	I
E	F#m	G#m	A	B	C#m	D#°	E

harmonized B scale with triads

I	ii	iii	IV	V	vi	vii°	I
B	C#m	D#m	E	F#	G#m	A#°	B

harmonized F# scale with triads

I	ii	iii	IV	V	vi	vii°	I
F#	G#m	A#m	B	C#	D#m	E#°	F#

harmonized C# scale with triads

I	ii	iii	IV	V	vi	vii°	I
C#	D#m	E#m	F#	G#	A#m	B#°	C#

harmonized F scale with triads

I	ii	iii	IV	V	vi	vii°	I
F	Gm	Am	Bb	C	Dm	E°	F

116

harmonized B♭ scale with triads

harmonized E♭ scale with triads

harmonized A♭ scale with triads

harmonized D♭ scale with triads

harmonized G♭ scale with triads

harmonized C♭ scale with triads

Page 85

MAJOR SCALES HARMONIZIED WITH SEVENTH CHORDS

harmonized G scale with sevenths

harmonized D scale with sevenths

harmonized A scale with sevenths

harmonized E scale with sevenths

harmonized B scale with sevenths

harmonized F# scale with sevenths

harmonized C♯ scale with sevenths

C♯maj7   D♯m7   E♯m7   F♯maj7   G♯7   A♯m7   B♯ø7   C♯maj7
Imaj7   ii m7   iii m7   IVmaj7   V7   vi m7   vii ø7   Imaj7

harmonized F scale with sevenths

Fmaj7   Gm7   Am7   B♭maj7   C7   Dm7   Eø7   Fmaj7
Imaj7   ii m7   iii m7   IVmaj7   V7   vi m7   vii ø7   Imaj7

harmonized B♭ scale with sevenths

B♭maj7   Cm7   Dm7   E♭maj7   F7   Gm7   Aø7   B♭maj7
Imaj7   ii m7   iii m7   IVmaj7   V7   vi m7   vii ø7   Imaj7

harmonized E♭ scale with sevenths

E♭maj7   Fm7   Gm7   A♭maj7   B♭7   Cm7   Dø7   E♭maj7
Imaj7   ii m7   iii m7   IVmaj7   V7   vi m7   vii ø7   Imaj7

harmonized A♭ scale with sevenths

A♭maj7   B♭m7   Cm7   D♭maj7   E♭7   Fm7   Gø7   A♭maj7
Imaj7   ii m7   iii m7   IVmaj7   V7   vi m7   vii ø7   Imaj7

harmonized D♭ scale with sevenths

D♭maj7   E♭m7   Fm7   G♭maj7   A♭7   B♭m7   Cø7   D♭maj7
Imaj7   ii m7   iii m7   IVmaj7   V7   vi m7   vii ø7   Imaj7

harmonized G♭ scale with sevenths

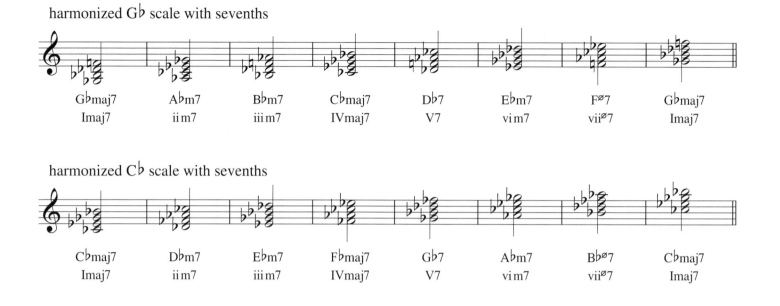

Gbmaj7	Abm7	Bbm7	Cbmaj7	Db7	Ebm7	Fø7	Gbmaj7
Imaj7	ii m7	iii m7	IVmaj7	V7	vi m7	viiø7	Imaj7

harmonized C♭ scale with sevenths

Cbmaj7	Dbm7	Ebm7	Fbmaj7	Gb7	Abm7	Bbø7	Cbmaj7
Imaj7	ii m7	iii m7	IVmaj7	V7	vi m7	viiø7	Imaj7

ABOUT THE AUTHOR

Chris Bowman is an experienced guitarist, teacher, and church musician. He owns the Instrumental Music Academy in north suburban Atlanta, where he oversees a dedicated staff of degree-holding instructors, all of whom are full-time musicians.

A classically trained guitarist, Chris has participated in two Grammy-nominated album projects. He is a Gold Record winning studio guitarist and has been guest guitarist with the Atlanta Pops Orchestra. He has appeared on *Entertainment Tonight* with CBS recording artists Buckner & Garcia. From 1972 to 1975, Chris toured and recorded with Dennis Yost & the Classics IV. (The band was inducted into the Georgia Music Hall of Fame in 1993.) From 1979 to 1990, Chris taught the Recording and Studio Production course at the Music Business Institute in Atlanta.

As a session player, Chris has performed on several record labels, including Columbia, Epic-Portrait, and Four-Star, as well as various independent labels. He has produced audio commercial jingles and industrial video soundtracks for Coca-Cola, Kroger, Tune-Up Clinic, Mazda World, Recline & Sleep stores, and others. Most recently, he played on the title track for the Disney/Pixar movie *Wreck-It Ralph* (2012).